THE SERVICE OF WOMEN IN THE CHURCH

The Service of Women in the Church

Dr. K. Deddens

The Service of Women in the Church
by Dr. K. Deddens
translated by Pieter H. Torenvliet

1st Edition, 2021

Library and Archives Canada Cataloguing in Publication

Title: The service of women in the Church / Dr. K. Deddens.
Names: Deddens, K., author.
Description: 1st edition.
Identifiers: Canadiana (print) 20210106344 | Canadiana (ebook) 20210106433 | ISBN 9780886661243
   (softcover) | ISBN 9780886661250 (HTML)
Subjects: LCSH: Women in Christianity. | LCSH: Women—Religious aspects—Christianity.
Classification: LCC BV639.W7 D43 2021 | DDC 270.082—dc23

Copyright © 2021 The Study. All rights reserved. No part of this publication may be reproduced in any manner without permission in writing from the publisher, except brief quotations used in connection with a review in a magazine or newspaper.

All Scripture quotations, unless otherwise indicated, are taken from the Holy Bible, NIV (2013)

All quotations from liturgical forms, confessions, and Psalms are taken from the *Book of Praise: Anglo-Genevan Psalter* (Winnipeg: Premier, 2014).

Design: @vanveenjf

Published by The Study
Box 445, Fergus, Ontario
Canada N1M 3E2
www.thestudy-books.com

ISBN 978-0-88666-124-3

Printed in Canada

Contents

	Foreword	7
	Translator's note	8
1.	Emancipation	
	Liberation	11
	The Image of God	12
2.	Male and Female He Created them	
	'In the Beginning'	17
	Distinction	19
3.	By Godly Ordinance or Destiny?	
	After the Fall	23
	Paganism	25
	Jews	26
4.	Some Women in the Old Testament	
	Israël	29
	The Daughters of Zelophehad	31
	Miriam	32
	Deborah	33
	Huldah	33
5.	Spiritual Maturity after Pentecost	
	Coming of Christ	37
	Acts 1	38
	Acts 2	38
	Galatians 3	39
	1 Corinthians 7	40

　　　　1 Peter 3 40
　　　　1 John 2 41
6. The Service of several women in Paul's letters
　　　　Euodia and Syntyche 43
　　　　Phoebe 44
　　　　Priscilla 44
　　　　Other women 45
7. A Contradiction in the Bible?
　　　　To Prophesy or to be Silent? 49
　　　　A Longing for Emancipation in Corinth 51
8. Other Developments with respect to the position of women
　　　　Prophetesses 55
　　　　Other examples of Women 56
　　　　Changes 58
　　　　Middle Ages 60
　　　　Reformation 61
　　　　Deformation 62
　　　　On the flip side 62
9. Offices in the Church for Women?
　　　　Not permitted 65
　　　　Admission 66
　　　　Time-bound 66
　　　　Making Distinctions 67
　　　　I Timothy 2 69
　　　　Offices 71
10. Voting Rights in the Church
　　　　Consequences 73
　　　　Argumentation 74
　　　　Before and after the election 75
　　　　Is voting exercising authority? 76
　　　　Cooperation 78
　　　　Not limited 80
11. Conclusion 83
12. For Reflection and Discussion 85

Foreword

AT least one half of the world's population consists of women; ergo, at least half of the church consists of women. Have you noticed? Only until recently, have women been permitted to embrace new and enlarged leadership roles in society, education, business, and politics. Within most orthodox and conservative churches, however, women have not been permitted into leadership roles. Though they teach and lead in Christian schools or lead businesses, in many Reformed churches not much has changed in the last century.

Many of the changes women and men have experienced, especially since WWII, have been unparalleled in the history of Western society. Unfortunately, the initiatives driving these changes often originated in secular circles and were motivated by feministic, humanistic and egalitarian principles. Accordingly, some of these changes were stiffly resisted by Christian church leaders: working outside of the home, equal pay for equal work, equal job security, equal professional opportunities. The list can be lengthened. As our Western culture changed, Christian churches often felt the need to be counter cultural. Gradually, however, most churches embraced the cultural shifts that permitted their female members with more freedom of choice. Some church denominations have even eliminated all barriers to women in leadership, replacing men in consistories, and on the pulpit. Not everyone is happy with these developments. Should there be limits to the service of women in our churches? If there are limits, what are they?

Dr. K. Deddens traces the history of the role of women in the midst of God's people from creation into the present time. Very often women became victims of their cultural context, also in the midst of God's people. Deddens clearly shows that God's people failed to listen to God's Word and instead they allowed the prevailing culture to dictate their attitudes and practices both in Israel (in the Old Testament) and in the church after Pentecost. In a world permeated by sin and selfishness, the motivation for emancipation has often been rooted in sin, but conversely, the motivation to refuse permission to women to employ their gifts and talents has also been rooted in sin and selfishness, sometimes under the guise of Biblical distinctives.

Dr. K. Deddens, with his substantial knowledge and experience, has provided his readers with an insightful story about women in service to the church. This story may leave you with many questions that need more discussion. Therefore, the last chapter of this book provides readers with opportunities to discuss these questions in the light of God's Word. Definitive solutions are not always available. In 1 Cor. 13:12, the apostle Paul states, "For now we see only a reflection as in a mirror; then we shall see face to face. Now I know in part; then I shall know fully, even as I am fully known." Also, in the context of women's service in the church we will be confronted with questions without clear answers. These discussions need humility, a willingness to listen to each other, to God's Word, and the guidance of the Holy Spirit.

May Dr. Deddens' book serve to give you a better understanding and appreciation for the gifts that God has bestowed on the church in both women and men.

Pieter H. Torenvliet

Translator's Note

The expression "lost in translation" captures a real problem. A quick Google check at the Biblegateway website will show you that the English Bible has been translated into more than 40 different versions! Clearly, it has been difficult to get everyone to agree what the best translation should be.

Though we cannot and will not compare the translation of this book to the difficulties of translating the Bible, the fact remains that we lose (some of) the original meaning in translation. Many people, familiar with the Dutch original, have read the final text of this book, and they agree that the intent and content of this book has been faithfully rendered into English.

More needs to be said. Dr. K. Deddens wrote this book in 1978 in the Netherlands. Interestingly, many of the contemporary issues that he discusses are still relevant today in our Anglo-Saxon Western societies. At the outset, however, it was determined that many of the references that Deddens used are not accessible today, at least, not in English. Furthermore, this translation was commissioned to focus on the needs of Reformed churches in Canada, the USA and Australia. Therefore, footnoting serves to clarify issues for those readers. All of the footnotes were written by the translator. Dr. Deddens had attempted to translate his book, but circumstances dictated that a new fresh translation was needed.

Obviously, Dr. Deddens (who passed-away in 2005) cannot be consulted, but his widow, Mrs. Deddens wanted to see her husband's wish fulfilled in having this book professionally translated. She also agreed that the text of the book would need some adaptation and timely clarification. Therefore, she provided permission to make these changes to the text to bring it up to date. The translator has not added any text. He did eliminate text that was dated and irrelevant to our current readers.

The last chapter that provides opportunities for additional reflection and discussion, are the collaborative work of the translator and Detmer Deddens, son of Dr. K. Deddens.

Pieter H. Torenvliet, Chilliwack
Detmer Deddens, Abbotsford

Note: To provide the reader with clear and accessible Scripture references, Bible quotations have been taken from the New International Version (2013), unless noted otherwise.

I. Emancipation

Liberation

Can any period throughout the history of humanity be more appropriately called the century of liberation than the 20th century? In the 19th century emancipation was remarkable: Western societies finally banned slavery, leading to the emancipation of tens of thousands of slaves in the Americas and in European colonies across the world. The consequences of this emancipation have reverberated forcefully up to the present time.

In the context of this book, however, I have focussed specifically on the emancipation of *women*, a momentous liberation movement that has been felt across *all* ethnicities. Let us not forget that this movement has impacted the most elementary relationships between two genders. Additionally, we can establish that the spirit of liberation of women has its roots in all kinds of liberation movements worldwide.

Especially in Western societies, for centuries, women have chafed at the submissive roles that were imposed upon them by men. But it was especially early in the 20th century that many people adamantly maintained that the slavery of women should be finally and effectively ended. Their imprisonment in the kitchen, the living room and in the bedroom had lasted far too long! Similar to the declarations of emancipation[1] of slaves in the 19th century, contemporary women should also be declared totally liberated, they proclaimed. The exclamation of the French Revolution, "Liberty, equality and fraternity!" should also, and equally, apply to

---

1. The governments of most Western countries declared slavery illegal during the 19th century, (British Empire, 1833; French colonies, 1834; Dutch colonies, 1862; U.S.A., 1863, etc.).

them. Women are humans, just like men, and therefore equal, for women must yield equal opportunities, equal freedoms, and equal rights.

At this point we would do well to observe how far we have actually come since the beginning of the previous century.[2] Today, however, advocates in our society demand much more: women should not feel compelled to be bound by the constraints of marriage and the responsibilities of motherhood; they must be *totally* free. The traditional views that marriage should be sacred and permanent are deemed to be the inventions of oppressors (i.e., men), who have enslaved women for many centuries claiming the support of various Bible references. Some writers even suggest that a feministic theology, comparable to liberation theology[3], should be developed to investigate and evaluate traditional theologies from a feministic perspective. Why? Because, they assert, traditional theology was developed by *men* and for *men*. Since the creation of Eve, who was created from a rib taken from Adam, up to today, Western religion has been a male dominated activity in which women were simply relegated to the service of men. Feministic theology is rooted in a skewed view which declares that women should be emancipated from all the oppressive structures in the church, the family and society.

Image of God

Contemporary feministic theologians maintain that we should embrace existential feminism. They suggest that only when feministic theology has demonstrated the alienating structures in theology, church and liturgy, then will women discover and embrace a new consciousness.

The image of the woman as presented in patriarchal male-dominated religion can no longer be accepted. In addition, the image of the male 'leader of Israel' is no longer deemed to be applicable. One of the most radical mid-century feminist theologians proclaimed that she wanted to completely "castrate" this image of exclusive male leadership[4] because this image was deemed to be an insult to women placing them in a secondary level of humanity. She asserted that this does not mean that 'god' would be defrocked. On the contrary, her 'god' would simply be neutered in terms of gender. This 'neutering' would concern a new creational

---

2. Many issues that we don't even consider as gender issues today were hotly contested during the first half of the 20th century: women's right to vote, ownership of property, equal pay for equal work, equal access to education at all levels, equal access to employment, etc.

3. Liberation theology arose especially in Latin America during the mid 20th century, advocating social justice for the oppressed and exploited poor. Jesus was often portrayed as a social revolutionary upbraiding the established powers of his day. This theology was aligned with socialist thinking and was employed to engage the Roman Catholic church to address the needs of the oppressed masses in Latin America.

4. De Beauvoir, Simone. Le deuxième Sexe I, II, Paris, 1949.

power that emanates from both god and the humans who seek a new ultimate meaning and a new reality of life.

Quite conspicuously, this feministic theologian consistently uses 'god' written with a lower case 'g', which is also typical of the thinking embraced by these revolutionary women. No longer is this 'faith' about the God and Father of our Lord Jesus Christ, but rather, about an idol, a product of their pagan thinking. As such, we could say that it's not about *'theology.'* Their gods are a product of their own imagination and they are enslaved to those things that by nature are not gods (Gal. 4:8-11). With the Galatian Christians, Paul was describing their former slavery. Sadly however, this modern thinking does not concern a rejected and an abandoned *past*, but rather, it is about a *future* which feministic theologians endorse and worship. They proclaim that this existential change in thinking must be the image of the future. The Biblical image of God must be replaced by the image that has evolved by feministic theology (i.e., an image or idol that people have shaped of God).

This so-called theology[5] is clearly consistent with the thinking rooted in the French Revolution, and was articulated by Simone de Beauvoir, the pagan partner of Jean-Paul Sartre[6]. Referring to the position of women, she wrote, "Legislators, priests, philosophers, writers and scholars have exerted an intense commitment to prove that the subordinate position of women was the will of heaven and that this subordination provided advantages on earth. The religions invented by men, mirror the will and the desire (of men) to rule: they drew their weaponry against women from the myths about Eve and Pandora".[7]

In Greek mythology, Pandora was believed to be the first woman on earth. Ancient Greeks claimed that Zeus, the king of the Olympian gods, had ordered that a woman should be created. Why? To become the undoing and misfortune of humanity![8] To facilitate this process, Zeus gave the woman a box that contains all kinds of evils, and commanded her never to open the box. Her curiosity, however, got the better of her, and she opened the box anyway (as Zeus had determined). When she opened the box, all kinds of evil, diseases and troubles flew out and spread over the face of the earth.

---

5. Dr. Deddens disparages de Beauvoir's thinking and writing as proper theology. Her 'god' is one of her own making, a god tailored to her feministic/humanistic and existentialistic imagination. There's no real relationship between this pagan thinking and a theology that focusses on the nature and work of the God in Scriptures.

6. Jean-Paul Sartre (1905-1980) French existentialist philosopher, embraced a philosophy acclaiming the freedom of the individual human being. His life-long partner was Simone de Beauvoir, the feminist theologian.

7. De Beauvoir, Simone. Le deuxième Sexe I, II, Paris, 1949.

8. According to Greek myths, man was created (from clay) by the Titan god, Prometheus, who subsequently also gave him fire. Zeus was not pleased.

de Beauvoir put this Pandora from Greek mythology on the same level as Eve, the "mother of all living", as God himself revealed in his Word. Moreover, in this latter story, the emancipated women claim, we are confronted with a myth that men have invented for their own benefit. If feminists today, however, – whether they claim to be theologians or not – attack God in his Being, in his image and essence of God, as he revealed at the time of creation, what then will people think about accepting the rest of God's revelation? Clearly, we must return to the *beginning* of Scriptures if we want to understand the service of women in the church.

Adam and Eve are driven from the garden of Eden.

2. Male and Female He created them

In the beginning

To understand the relationship between men and women properly, the Scriptures themselves direct us to look at the beginning, i.e., creation. I'll choose three examples. When the prophet Malachi condemns unfaithfulness in marriage, he poses the question: "Do we not all have one Father? Did not one God create us?" In the latter context he asks, "Why do we profane the covenant of our ancestors by being unfaithful to one another?" (Mal. 2:10)

When the Pharisees wanted to test Jesus, they asked him whether husbands can divorce their wives for all kinds of reasons. The Saviour replies, "Haven't you read… that at the beginning the Creator made them male and female, . . ?" (Matt. 19:4)

Finally, when the apostle Paul writes about the place of women in the congregation and about their relationship to their husbands, he writes to Timothy: "For Adam was formed first, then Eve" (1 Tim. 2:13). Following the examples given in Scripture, we must also go back to the beginning when God created mankind.

In the beginning, Adam was alone as human being. God had given him the garden of Eden to live where the LORD presented him with a marvelous variety of life. When Adam was created from the dust of the earth, there were already all kinds of animals and other kinds of living creatures. But the man, Adam, was exceptional in that he was alone in creation and he was the only one who had been created in God's image and after his likeness. He gave names to all the animals, "but for Adam no suitable helper was found" (Gen. 1:20). That is a striking comment in Scripture which pictures Adam as *needy*. The word that is used to express "helper" is also expressed in the name "Ebenezer" – stone of help. It points to help which God himself provides, though it may come via a specific way. There is – regardless of the exalted position man was given – a kind of disappointment and a kind of yearning; you could also translate this passage: "But for Adam there was not found a helper fit for him" (ESV) or no "other half."

But that disappointment is abolished by God and he accommodates the need of that longing:

> So the Lord God caused the man to fall into a deep sleep; and while he was sleeping, he took one of the man's ribs and then closed up the place with flesh. Then the Lord God made a woman from the rib he had taken out of the man, and he brought her to the man.
> The man said,
> "This is now bone of my bones
> and flesh of my flesh;
> she shall be called 'woman,'
> *for she was taken out of man."* (Gen. 2: 21-23)

Adam sings about his joy and expresses thankfulness that his disappointment was taken away and that his desire had been fulfilled. He had received a woman and wife from God's hand, or we could also say that he received a companion of his similitude or likeness.

That is the first thing we must establish here: Adam received a companion that was just like him. The man, who had felt incomplete and needy, received the 'other half.' The woman was created as bone of his bone and flesh of his flesh. In other words, he received someone who was a perfect 'fit' with him as a co-dependant, corresponding to him as an equivalent counterpart who met with all his needs. She was not Adam's slave whom he could treat in whatever way he wished; nor was she a lower creation who had to jump to do his will. No, she was his companion, as *ishah* (woman) is the counterpart to *ish* (man).

Adam received a valuable gift from God, a gift with whom he could safeguard and develop the beautiful garden of Eden, and a gift with whom he could develop culture in the world.

Together, they were now complete. Consequently, in his wedding song Adam sang about being one flesh, bound together in the most sublime and greatest unity possible. They are joined together, and together they formed a totality that is greater than the sum of the parts.

Distinction

In the beginning already, Scripture points to the equivalence of man and woman and the unity that they form together. Having established that fact, however, not everything has been said. It is significant that man was created first, and it is equally significant that the woman was taken from the man. This signifies a form of order: Adam is created first and afterwards, Eve, his wife. The man precedes. Some people have questioned whether this creational sequence should be followed by a certain order in standing, a hierarchy as it were. Some have suggested that man is the crown of creation, since he is finally created on the sixth day after all the other creatures had been created. They conclude that there should be a difference in order, a higher order in standing for man, since Eve was created even later than Adam. That only *appears* to be a logical conclusion. In Genesis 1:26 a clear 'intrusion' can be observed. A separate decision appeared to be necessary to create the crown of creation. Dr. H. Bavinck[1] once explained that God created man in the wake of a very special consultation and decision. Scriptures provide irrefutable proof of that process: as first human, Adam is created as the crown of all of creation that preceded him. Initially Adam lived alone as human. Only afterwards did God fulfill man's desire that he would not be left alone. God provided a help and counterpart for man. The help that God provided is equivalent, but she *follows* Adam's creation. Like Adam, she is created in God's image, but she *follows* Adam. The man precedes, and that sequence is unchangeable.

In the New Testament, this order of creation is highlighted several times. Think in this latter context of 1 Tim. 2:13. Here Paul writes about the worship service. In this chapter he first discusses the proper place of prayer in the worship service and subsequently, the apostle focusses on a second important element, the teaching in the context of worship. When the teaching takes place, women are to remain silent because that teaching in the congregation bears a special character, that is, speaking with authority. Teaching is a unique exercise of leadership according to Paul, which also includes leadership over other men, a form of leadership that has not been given to women.

Paul posits a special motivation to embrace this view as it is rooted in the order of creation as revealed by God himself: first Adam was created, and then Eve. For

---

1. Dr. Herman Bavinck (1854-1921) was a Dutch Reformed theologian. Initially, he was professor of dogmatics at the Reformed Theological Seminary in Kampen. In 1902, he became Professor of Theology at the Free University in Amsterdam. His Reformed Dogmatics (4 volumes) was translated into many languages, also into English, and is still considered an authoritative source today.

that reason, that special exercise of authority and leadership does not rest with the woman, but with the man. Man leads, he precedes the woman because God created him first. In this way, the Holy Spirit, as Author of Scripture, provides a connection between the Old and New Testaments; Genesis 1 and 2 are connected to 1 Timothy 2. Woman, having been created equivalent to man, is tasked to work together with man to work the garden and to safeguard it. Together they share responsibility for this cultural mandate.

Note: woman is not created as the subordinate of man or his slave. No, she is his life partner, his counterpart, the one created to fit with him, his co-worker. Having emphatically established this unique equivalence, it must still be emphasized as well that there is a difference in ranking. Man, as created first, precedes as he continues in the task with which he was already occupied when God brought Eve to him. God himself designated this order. At the outset, God established a relational order, Adam first and afterward his help-meet; this order will be determinative for their future together. This relationship is not to be understood as competing genders, but rather, as a harmonious cooperation of man and woman in which the distinction between them is not levelled or negated. Rather, it is to be a relationship wherein man, who is given leadership, is first among equals. If that order is reversed, however, and woman assumes leadership over the man, there will be a catastrophe. History bears that out.

A woman receiving the host at Eucharist.

3. By Godly ordinance or by Chance?

After the Fall

In the previous chapter, we emphasized that God created the woman equivalent to the man. When Genesis 1 states that God created man[1] "in our image, in our likeness" (vs.26), it immediately follows with the words, "male and female he created them" (vs.27). Clearly, that means that also woman was created in the image of God, and not as a lesser or secondary creature. She was created as a creature fully equivalent to man, as the help-meet for Adam. Therefore, God said, "I will make him a helper fit for him" (Gen. 2:18, ESV). You can also translate this expression as follows: "help as his counterpart, a help that is close by, or, a help that is on par with him." Think of these translations in context of the fact that woman's creation eliminated him from being alone. At the same time, she was a form of help that would fit with him, fit his need and provide him someone whom he could truly consider being together with him.

Being together, as man and woman, however, there was still a clear distinction. Remember: man had been created first, and then the woman. Leadership had been entrusted to the man, but woman chose to usurp this leadership. Though man and woman had stood together in God's covenant and had been crowned with honour and glory to carry God's blessing if they would obey the LORD's commands, the woman when she was tempted by the devil, chose a different course that would lead away from God. Instead of choosing the way of

---

1. The NIV (2013) translation bears this out clearly: Then God said, "Let us make mankind in our image, in our likeness", vs. 26, and again, "So God created mankind in his own image, in the image of God he created them;
male and female he created them." (vs. 27). In vs. 28, we read: "God blessed them and said to them, 'Be fruitful and increase in number.'" (Using the plural: them)

righteousness with her husband, she chose a self-willed course diametrically against God's commandment. A second corruption followed: the woman gave the forbidden fruit to her husband, and he also ate the fruit.

What a disaster followed immediately after their disobedience! All their relationships are broken, also the relationship between the two of them. Note that the woman blamed the serpent, and the man quickly distances himself from his wife. Instead of the wedding song he had sung earlier, a bitter complaint comes from his lips: "The woman whom you gave to be with me, she gave me fruit of the tree, and I ate" (Gen. 3: 12).

In response to their disobedience, God declared how the relationship between the man and his wife would be transformed[2]

> To the woman he said,
> "I will surely multiply your pain in childbearing;
> in pain you shall bring forth children.
> Your desire shall be contrary to your husband,
> but he shall rule over you."
> And to Adam he said,
> "Because you have listened to the voice of your wife
> and have eaten of the tree
> of which I commanded you,
> 'You shall not eat of it,'
> cursed is the ground because of you;
> in pain you shall eat of it all the days of your life;
> thorns and thistles it shall bring forth for you;
> and you shall eat the plants of the field.
> By the sweat of your face *you shall eat bread.*
> (Gen. 3: 16-19, ESV)

---

[2]. Dr. Deddens comments that in the wake of the curse that the Lord pronounced over woman, many people concluded subsequently that God had actually formulated a command to the woman that she must simply obey her husband as lord and master, bereft of any will of her own. That attitude was certainly the situation women experienced from ancient times up to the present in many cultures. Also, in some Christian circles, wives are/were believed to be little more than chattels of their husbands to conform with the curse God proclaimed over Eve's disobedience. In his ministry, Jesus clearly provided us with a much different attitude and behaviour.

The fact that Christian women are no longer a form of "property" (i.e., without a will of their own) is not to be seen as a disregard of God's command, but a proper softening of their lot. That our (Western) women are free from many of the shackles that still bind Eastern women is not a sin, but grace. The history of the world is replete with the indignities that have been thrust upon women. That was their lot foretold by the LORD on account of the curse that resulted from the woman's sin of rebellion. But the LORD did not command this as a moral law or injunction. (Cf. A Jansen, (1923), Eva's Dochters)

Paganism

In the centuries following the fall into sin, a heavy hand of dominion fell, so that women suffered significant adversity and obstacles regardless of the direction they chose to go, consistent with the words the LORD had spoken (Gen. 3:16). After the fall into sin, all over the world, women would be confronted with this often brutal and uncompromising lot in life, bereft of a voice or a will of her own, frequently suffering the indignity of a tyrant husband or master, relegated to the level of living merchandise or the object of basic lust. During ancient history, among pagans, most people believed women had no rights, and could only find safety or security under the care of a father, her parents, or her husband. In China, for example, women were clearly inferior to men. The Chinese philosopher, Confucius, had nothing but derogatory remarks about women. In India, Buddhism also allotted women to inferior positions under men.

Ancient Egyptians embraced oral marriages, (i.e., a simple verbal arrangement), and divorce was a one-sided affair controlled by men. In Greece, the birth of a girl was often an unhappy event that frequently left girls exposed to the elements. If they lived, they were relegated to the women quarters and married off to the highest bidder. When the girl was married, she was completely subject to the will and whim of her husband, who was usually significantly older than she was. Double standards, certainly from today's perspective, were normal. If a girl or woman committed adultery, she was punished severely or even killed. Men, on the other hand, were usually free to do what they wanted, especially if it concerned visits to the *hetaerae*, which were basically prostitutes.

In many societies, polygamy was common, as were various forms of prostitution, concubinage with slaves, and the trading or lending out of wives. Later on, formal bigamy became commonplace.

In Greece, the primary purpose of marriage was generating children in the interest of the state. Abortion was not seen as an evil and was sometimes a recommended course of action. Not until a newborn had drawn his first breath was he considered to be human. In Sparta, for example, fathers had the right to abandon their newborn, especially if it was a girl or a boy who appeared to be weak or sickly. Often the city fathers would make this decision. The philosopher, Plato, actually believed that women were less inclined to be virtuous than men. Another philosopher, Aristotle, considered women intellectually and morally inferior to men. The dramatist, Euripides, is portrayed as a woman hater in his dramas; Hesiod, the author of Greek mythologies, claims women are a calamity for mortals, and Meander, another writer, labelled women as the greatest of beasts or monsters. In a public speech, the Greek statesman Demosthenes declared, "We have the *hetaerae* (or *hetaera*) for our pleasure, concubines for our daily physical needs, and our spouses to generate legal children, and as faithful guardians over our household."

In ancient Roman society, their oldest laws declared that the *pater familias*, or father of the family, had complete legal control over his family. Though marriage was officially monogamous, all kinds of sexual decadence became quite common in Roman society. In many circles, concubinage became common in the place of marriage.

Divorce became increasingly common so that eventually a simple verbal declaration of divorce was good enough to end a marriage. A man could divorce because his wife was barren or because she had ventured outside without a head covering. Abortion, abandonment, infanticide and the sale of children for prostitution were common. Frequenting prostitutes was not a problem. In the final years of the Roman empire, decadence was rife, to the point that many historians ascribe the fall of the empire to this decadence.

Jews

In the countries around Israel people were clearly polytheists and polygamists. But also in Israel, the prophets tell us that the position of women in Israel, just before the time of the New Testament, was very insecure. Sons were preferred over daughters: "Congratulations to him whose children are men, woe to him whose children are daughters." During and after the Babylonian exile, marriages were solemnized by means of a contract that determined all the financial conditions.

Once young women were married, they became the property of their husbands: he is the lord and master (baal); she is simply a piece of property. If she received children, she received a degree of respect as mother, especially if sons had been born. Childless women were vulnerable to mockery and disdain. Also, in Jewish law there was clear evidence of a double standard: divorce for men was much easier than for women. Often they would appeal to Deut. 24:1 - "When a man takes a wife and marries her, if then she finds no favor in his eyes because he has found some indecency in her, and he writes her a certificate of divorce and puts it in her hand and sends her out of his house, and she departs out of his house ..." The one rabbinical school taught that the only reason for divorce was adultery, but another school taught that if she had burned the meal, or served a meal that was too salty, a man could divorce his wife. Rabbi Akiva gave permission to divorce if a woman was caught eating in the street, and he consented with divorce if a man had found a more beautiful woman. Many quotations are available that demonstrate expressions of disdain and the inferiority of women.

Women eat like gluttons, are nosey listeners, are slow and lazy.
Many women; much witchcraft.
Those who talk a lot to women, inherit hell.

In a Jewish book of prayer, there is a lot of praise similar to that also found among pagans: "Blessed are you, O God, that you did not make me a heathen, a slave of a woman".

Through studies of the Torah, specifically the doctrines concerning circumcision, the belief arose after the Babylonian exile that women were considered to be similar to slaves and children. Blame for the fall into sin was laid exclusively on women. They were also believed to be especially vulnerable to sorcery and superstition. Even the fall of the angels was blamed on women! At a funeral, women were expected to walk at the front of the procession because they were blamed for bringing death into the world. Special worship services for women were not organized, but they were allowed into synagogue worship, albeit in a special place reserved for them, separated from the men. Though they were officially allowed to hear the reading of the Torah, in practice, however, it appeared that this was not allowed. Women were not allowed to swear an oath. Rabbi Eliezer declared, "It is better to burn the Tora than to give it into the hands of a woman." From all sides, in pagan societies and in Jewish society "when the set time had fully come" (Galatians 4: 4-7[3]), women lived under the ironclad lordship and tyranny of men.

---

3. Galatians 4: 4-7. "But when the set time had fully come, God sent his Son, born of a woman, born under the law, to redeem those under the law, that we might receive adoption to sonship."

Women in the medieval monastic world, their last redoubt in a diaconal ministry.

4. Women in the Old Testament

Israel

When we compare the *official* and *Biblical* position of women in Israel to those in pagan societies, there was to be a great difference. In contrast to the *human* laws which the pagan rulers promulgated to regulate and prescribe the worship of their idols, the people of Israel recognized a divine Lawgiver who established a covenant with his holy people, Israel.

He has revealed his word to Jacob,
his laws and decrees to Israel.
He has done this for no other nation;
they do not know his laws. (Ps. 147:19)

It is also very evident in Israel that the paradisal harmony and relationships were in turmoil, also the relationships in marriage. When the Pharisees asked Jesus about divorce, our Lord answered, "Moses permitted you to divorce your wives because your hearts were hard. But it was not this way from the beginning" (Matt. 19:8).

Polygamy was normal among the people of the surrounding nations; their kings acquired large harems of wives and concubines. Did Israel shun this male indulgence? The Bible shows us that it didn't. They followed the bad example of the pagan neighbours. But Scripture also shows us what a lot of grief this custom created. The bitter rivalries between Leah and Rachel as they competed for their husband's love and attention, or Hannah and Penninah, the wives of Elkanah. Deuteronomy 17 clearly commanded that a king "must not take many wives, or his heart will be led astray" (vs. 17). When Solomon chose to rebel against this command, it contributed to his downfall.

Scripture describes rights and privileges that a woman and wife in Israel had, in contrast to the pagan societies where women and wives were not accorded any more rights than an adopted daughter. In Israel the woman was to be honoured as wife and mother. Think of the Law as recorded in Exodus 20 and Deut. 5. The fifth commandment directs every covenant child, personally, to honour *father* and *mother*. Both parents are placed in one line. Children must *honour* their parents; that is, respect them, bow under their authority. Note the contrast with the Babylonian-Assyrian wisdom literature where we read, "Whoever fails to honour his *father*, will soon suffer calamity." In his wisdom, our God emphasizes that *both* parents, father *and* mother, are to be honoured and respected.

In the book of Proverbs, we find numerous references that underscore this command. The disrespectful attitude of a child toward both his mother and father is condemned.

> "He who does violence to his father and chases away his mother is a son who brings shame and reproach" (19:26, ESV).
>
> "If one curses his father or his mother, his lamp will be put out in utter darkness" (20:20, ESV).
>
> "The eye that mocks a father and scorns to obey a mother will be picked out by the ravens of the valley and eaten by the vultures" (30:17, ESV).

Quite clearly, women in Israel had rights. When a man committed adultery, in other nations he would be left free, completely. But the LORD emphatically tells his people that he hates divorce and that the punishment for adultery is *death* for both men and women. From a positive side, it must be noted that women were to be integrally involved in Israel's religious practices. During worship and sacrifice, women were involved. They were present during prayer and sacrificial meals. When the Law was read to Israel, they joined the men in the audience. "Assemble the people—men, women and children, and the foreigners residing in your towns—so they can listen and learn to fear the Lord your God and follow carefully all the words of this law" (Deut. 31:12). In Nehemiah we read, "Ezra the priest brought the Law before the assembly, which was made up of men and women and all who were able to understand" (8:2). "He read it aloud from daybreak till noon as he faced the square before the Water Gate in the presence of the men, women and others who could understand. And all the people listened attentively to the Book of the Law" (8:3).

In Old Testament times, women participated in the celebration of the Passover, and at Pentecost they joined the family when they went to Jerusalem to celebrate the first fruits of the harvest and the giving of the Law. In their homes and throughout Israel, women were integral to the fellowship of the covenant. Additionally, the women were involved in many of the cultic activities in and around the temple: they played musical instruments and danced at great festive celebrations. During the days of Nehemiah and Ezra they participated in the temple choir to sing God's praise. From all of the above, it is abundantly clear that women were completely involved in worship activities throughout the Old Testament.

Daughters of Zelophehad

The story about the daughters of Zelophehad (Numbers 27, 36) has a special place in Scripture. Zelophehad belonged to the tribe of Manasseh, but he had died without male heirs. He did have five daughters. Because there were no male heirs, the daughters were afraid that their family would die out in the midst of Israel when the conquered land would be divided among the tribes. Therefore, they went to Moses with a request, "Give us property among our father's relatives" (27:4). Moses brought the matter before the LORD who answered, "What Zelophehad's daughters are saying is right. You must certainly give them property as an inheritance among their father's relatives and give their father's inheritance to them" (vs. 7).

Some people have asserted that the daughters of Zelophehad should be seen as the earliest successful contestants for women's rights. But that conclusion is inappropriate. They did not champion personal rights or their rights as women. The place of their family and clan in the midst of Israel was at stake. In Numbers 36, however, we read that the heads of families from the tribe of Manasseh were concerned about marriages with these daughters if they would contract marriages with men outside of their tribe. Then their inheritance would potentially go to another tribe and be lost to Manasseh. Therefore, Moses commanded, "What the tribe of the descendants of Joseph is saying is right. This is what the Lord commands for Zelophehad's daughters: They may marry anyone they please as long as they marry within their father's tribal clan" (36:6).

What did this command mean? Marriage of daughters was made completely subordinate to the lot of their inheritance, the name of her father. Therefore, the daughters of Zelophehad would inherit the land, with the proviso that they would marry within their tribe. If they would not, in the grand scheme of the matter, this would have meant that Zelophehad would not have shared in the future of the Messiah, the true inheritance. Their marriages were subordinate to maintaining the inheritance rights of their father. In the context of our 'story', we see that women are honoured in their position in the midst of Israel, God's covenant people of the Old Testament. This issue has nothing to do with our modern perceptions of emancipation.

The Old Testament church is replete with examples of exceptional women. Therefore, I will restrict myself to a few choices. These choices are not meant to suggest that *every* woman in Israel received a position and responsibility such as men, or that the LORD had not given official leadership in the Old Testament only to men. These examples are not to be misconstrued as typical women in Israel's history. It was very clear, however, that the Lord made women to serve in the coming of the Messiah. Isn't women's primordial mother Eve not called "the mother of all living"? Were they not also given gifts, talents, and services to use concretely for the continuation of God's work in this world?

MIRIAM

In Exodus 15 we read that Miriam led the women in singing a song of praise of deliverance to the LORD. But that is not the only important service we may attribute to Moses' sister. Through the Holy Spirit she also sings herself in response to the others.

> Then Miriam the prophet, Aaron's sister, took a timbral in her hand, and all the women followed her, with timbrels and dancing.
> Miriam sang to them:
> "Sing to the Lord,
> for he is highly exalted.
> Both horse and driver
> he has hurled into the sea." (*Ex. 15: 20, 21*)

Much later, the prophet Micah names Miriam in the same breath as her brothers, Moses and Aaron, when he describes the Lord's deliverance of his people:

> I brought you up out of Egypt
> and redeemed you from the land of slavery.
> I sent Moses to lead you,
> also Aaron and Miriam. (*Micah 6:4*)

Miriam's service to the Lord was important, but certainly not as an emancipation as if she was given a special voice in her covenant community in the Old Testament. Over against this important service, we are also reminded of an instructive event in Numbers 12. This same Miriam was severely censured because of her behaviour. Together with her brother Aaron they challenged Moses, "Has the Lord spoken only through Moses?... Hasn't he also spoken through us?'" (Num. 12:2). Miriam was punished and stricken with leprosy so that she had to be banished outside the camp for seven days, cast out of God's people.

DEBORAH

Deborah is another unique woman in the history of salvation. Some people would like to depict her as an advocate of women's emancipation, long before anyone had given this any thought. This was simply not the case. At that time there was no man willing or able to lead and judge Israel, so Deborah arises as prophetess. From her house under the palm trees on Ephraim's mountains, the Holy Spirit used her to lead the people of Israel with the *Word of God*. She was not a proud, fiery, independent and strong woman – an Amazon,[1] as it were. She is *simply* described as the wife of Lippidoth.

God's choice is completely consistent with the time of the judges; God ordains a weak woman, a man's wife (his 'subject'), to deliver Israel. The left-handed Ehud, an insignificant Gideon (Judges 6: 15), a bastard Jephthah, an undisciplined Samson, are also used by the LORD to deliver. Those that are weak in themselves are chosen to shame the strong!

Clearly, the prophetess Deborah is consistent with God's choices elsewhere. Also consider the fact that Deborah, a woman, prophesized – that *she* was ordained to speak God's word to the people – should have led the men to hide their heads in shame! This calling was not to serve as a point of personal honour because it was *God's gift*. Her calling as prophetess had nothing to do with her personal attributes such as wisdom or independence. But it came simply because she was chosen to speak God's word.

When Barak was commanded to lead Israel in battle, Deborah did not issue this command on her personal authority; it came as God's command. In all of this, it is evident that Deborah did not function as an emancipated woman, but a faithful woman who had received a revelation from the Lord. As we see in this story, God can choose women as his instrument to shame the men.

HULDAH

Also the prophetess Hulda (2 Kings 22: 14 – 20) who lived during the time of the god-fearing King Josiah, was no champion of emancipation. She was the wife of

---

1. In Greek mythology, the Amazons were a tribe of warrior women.

Shallum, keeper of the king's wardrobe. Five leading men - among others, Hilkiah the priest - go to her to ask her concerning the welfare of Jerusalem. The LORD uses Huldah to announce the punishment and evil that will come over Jerusalem on account of all her idolatries. She was also permitted to prophesy that the king would not see or experience this because he had humbled himself before the Lord.

As shown above, the Lord used women throughout the Old Testament, women who were also married and thus were subject to their husbands. God uses these women to use their gifts in service to the coming of his Son, Jesus Christ. When Samuel is born, God prompts Hannah so that she sings about God's deliverance. Many centuries later, in the wake of Gabriel's announcement, the words of Hannah's song are fulfilled in the song of praise by Mary when she sings about the birth of Jesus.

These women were not chattels or slaves, but neither were they champions of emancipation. They were ordained to *serve* in the coming of our Lord, Jesus Christ. It was this service that typified these women in the Old Testament.

The woman washing Jesus' feet.

5. Spiritual Maturity - Pentecost

The coming of the Christ

Jesus Christ came into this world to fulfill the law of God. He did not radically eliminate the law; he radically underscored the law. He did remove the curse of the law. That also applies to the seventh commandment and the whole relationship between men and women.

These relationships were restored to honour by the Lord. At a time that women were insignificant, Jesus did not consider himself too exalted to speak with them. Think, for example, about the conversation our Saviour had with the Samaritan woman. Mary and Martha spoke with him about the kingdom of heaven, and he even permits the latter to address him publicly while he was still on the road. Jesus permits a woman who was accused of sin to wash his feet. In his parables as well, the Lord frequently referenced women and holds them up as example.

By and large, even at Jesus' birth, men are left in the background. Two women, Mary and Elizabeth greet Jesus' imminent birth with great joy. Then at Jesus' presentation at the temple, we read not only about the joy and praise of Simeon, but also the very old Anna, a prophetess, praised God and spoke about the deliverance that he would bring to everyone in Jerusalem who awaited this redemption.

Who are the first witnesses of Jesus' resurrection? *Women* not only witness his resurrection first, but they are also the first to actually proclaim this gospel to the disciples.

Through Jesus' coming and his work of redemption, the Saviour has removed the curse that had rested on women since the fall into sin. Christ not only removed and bridled the tyranny men had over women, he liberated them; they possess freedom in God, through Jesus Christ. This is not an unbridled freedom of a revolutionary emancipation rooted in the devil, but rather, it is a unique liberty that allows them to follow Christ in his beautiful service.

Woman, who tempted the first Adam, may now follow the second Adam unburdened by the curse, to serve him with her gifts, especially with the love of her heart and her faith in the Lord. No less than man, the woman who follows Christ may share in the benefits of his atonement. Beside the man, she receives a place in the congregation of Christ. She shares in the same baptism and she sits with the men at the same Lord's Supper. Together they struggle in the same challenges of faith. That is the image of liberty, of freedom from the curse of sin; it is the image Scripture gives of the woman when Christ ascended to heaven and poured out his Spirit on Pentecost.

Acts 1

That story of liberation began already in Acts 1. When the disciples returned from the Mount of Olives to Jerusalem, and joined together in prayer, there were also women in their midst. Among others, we read about Mary, the mother of Jesus. But Luke expressly mentions that there are other women among them as well and that "they all joined together constantly in prayer, along with the women and Mary the mother of Jesus, and with his brothers" (Acts 1: 14).

"In those days" (vs. 15), Peter stood up and assumes the leadership among the brothers. The Greek word, "in those days" points to the close relationship to the events immediately preceding. These are the days during which the disciples continued in prayer for the Holy Spirit. There are about 120 people together. When he addresses the *brothers* he actually directs his attention to **all** the people, including the women. Frequently, the Scriptures speak about "brothers", using the male gender, without mentioning the women[1]. Also, the sisters are clearly integral to those who are addressed. The sisters are also part of the 120 people who pray, as they draw a lot to choose Matthias as an apostle, filling the vacancy left by Judas Iscariot.

Acts 2

Pentecost! Everybody is together again, not only the twelve apostles, but the whole congregation, men and women. *Everyone* is filled with the Holy Spirit, with no exceptions. Consistent with this general pouring out of the Spirit, Peter's sermon becomes a confirmation and fulfillment of the prophecies of Joel:

---

1. In Greek, Paul often uses the word "adelphoi" which, can refer to siblings in a family, men or women or both men and women (brothers and sisters) in the church. Many English translations, however, simply translate "men".

> And afterward,
> I will pour out my Spirit on all people.
> Your sons and daughters will prophesy,
> your old men will dream dreams,
> your young men will see visions.
> Even on my servants, both men and women,
> I will pour out my Spirit in those days. *(2:28, 29)*

The *leadership* in the apostolic church was clearly entrusted to the apostles. They are the witnesses who must proclaim the salvation of Jesus Christ. This work, however, is carried out with the full engagement of the congregation. It is fully able because it has reached Spiritual maturity, it is a congregation of both men and women, brothers and sisters in the Lord.

GALATIANS 3

Equipped (gifted) with their spiritual maturity given by the Spirit on Pentecost, men and woman work *together* in faith. In that same spirit of collaboration Paul addresses the Galatians concerning the unity and equality in Christ:

> So in Christ Jesus you are all children of God through faith, for all of you who were baptized into Christ have clothed yourselves with Christ. There is neither Jew nor Gentile, neither slave nor free, nor is there male and female, for you are all one in Christ Jesus. (Gal. 3:26-28)

The apostle writes about a lack of distinction, naming three ironclad distinctions common in the world of his day. In the congregation of Jesus Christ, however, the Jew has no advantage over the Greek, the free-born has nothing over the slave, and a man cannot exercise any rights over the woman. A man, simply because of his gender, does not have a more generous or beautiful place in the kingdom of God.

Here Paul does not preach a false equality such as some people maintain today. He does not say that ethnic differences are not meaningful, that national citizenship and cultural traditions are silly or foolish. Moreover, in expressing these views in this letter, the apostle does not provide a warrant for social upheaval, revolutionary unrest, or promote a liberation movement. Nor does he want to undermine or depreciate the distinctions that God established between the different genders. On the contrary, he declares that access to God's grace is equally and generously available for both men and women. Both men and women are God's cherished children, *one* in the Lord Jesus Christ.

1 Corinthians 7

Paul's writing is sharply critical of the disparagement and disregard of women in his day! In several of the letters that Paul wrote[2], we see a similar concern in promoting the equality in faith between men and women. In 1 Corinthians 7 where the apostle responds to several questions about marriage, he says, "For the unbelieving husband has been sanctified through his wife, and the unbelieving wife has been sanctified through her believing husband. Otherwise your children would be unclean, but as it is, they are holy" (1 Cor. 7:14). Paul states that also in the matter he discusses, a man is not to be placed above the woman when it concerns God's covenant. That covenant maintains its validity for posterity even though only one of them, man or woman, believe in the salvation in Jesus Christ. Regardless which one it is, the man does not have any advantage over the woman. In both cases, whether it is the faith of the man (husband) alone, or the faith of the woman (wife) alone, the children fall under the force of God's promises.

1 Peter 3

The apostle Peter echoes the same sentiment when he discusses marriage: "Husbands, in the same way be considerate as you live with your wives, and treat them with respect as the weaker partner and as heirs with you of the gracious gift of life, so that nothing will hinder your prayers." (1 Pet. 3: 7)

The men are forbidden to exasperate their wives, despise or disdain them or treat them like slaves. Wives are co-heirs of eternal life. Just like men, they have been bought from the power of Satan with the price of Christ's blood. Just like men, they have been delivered from perdition by God's grace. If men disregard or debase the facts of God's grace with respect to their wives, they create an impasse, a hindrance for prayer (i.e., that these prayers won't be received before God's throne of grace where they may be heard).

---

2. The message of the gospel is subversive: it goes against the sentiments and attitudes in society. Consequently, the message of the gospel is often counter-cultural. Interestingly, this aspect of the gospel is not unique to the New Testament. God had challenged Israel to be counter-cultural as well so that the freedom and harmony created by faithful adherence to the Law would be a sign to all the surrounding nations that Israel was unique, blessed, because their covenant God, Yahweh, is unique. Where God's grace abounds, people live in harmony. Deut. 4: 6-8; Ps. 147: 20.
Paul argues that faith in Christ creates a unique unity so that men and women stand as equals before God. That was also completely counter-cultural in Paul's day. The apostle extends this unity and uniqueness to the marriage relationship before God. When women heard the gospel and understood the implications of living in faith, this message must have sounded foreign, albeit, wonderful. What Paul writes, for example, in Eph. 5: 25-33, or what Peter writes in 1 Peter 3: 7, must have sounded like music in the ears of women. The gospel turns pagan culture on its ear. It does the same today in our post-Christian era.

1 John 2

One in faith, without any distinction between genders. John writes his first letter to his 'children' – i.e., both men and women! "But you have an anointing from the Holy One, and all of you know the truth" (1 John 2:5). Both men *and* women are clothed with the spiritual maturity bestowed upon them through the Holy Spirit. They have *all* received this anointing.

John writes this message to them antithetically against the anti-Christians of his day. He says, "They went out from us, but they did not really belong to us" (1 Jn. 2: 19). Over against this he states, "But you have an anointing from the Holy One, and all of you know the truth" (vs. 20). In other words: you may share in the anointing of the Spirit, and you may carry the truth.

The faithful men and women may confess God's name as we also read in the Heidelberg Catechism, L.D. 12. ". . . I am a member of Christ by faith and thus share in his anointing so that I may as prophet confess his name, as priest present myself a living sacrifice of thankfulness to him, and as king fight with a free and good conscience against sin and the devil in this life. . ."

We see that our confession repeats what Scriptures declare: in faith, men and women stand shoulder to shoulder. Both are given the privilege to fight the good fight of faith, both are called to confess God's name publicly, both men and women are obligated to use their gifts in his service. God's covenant provides us with the noble honour and riches that men and women may devote themselves together, faced with the same obligations of the covenant, and work under the blessing of that same covenant!

Rembrandt - The meeting of Mary and Elizabeth. -Luke 1:39-56

As evening approaches, Mary has completed a long journey, arriving at the house of Zechariah and Elizabeth. Here she greets her old cousin on the terrace in front of their house. The old Zechariah, still speechless because of his unbelief, joins them, leaning on the shoulder of a boy while a servant girl helps Mary take her travel garment off.

Rembrandt lets the eye focus on the women. Elizabeth appears piously reverent as she looks upon the noble face of Mary. She's pleasantly surprised and says: "But why am I so favored, that the mother of my Lord should come to me?"

She honours Mary because she recognizes her as the mother of her Lord. In Mary's appearance she notices how difficult it is for her to bear something so awesome, that she should become the mother of the Saviour of the world. In humility Elizabeth continues, "Blessed is she who has believed that the Lord would fulfill his promises to her!"

6. THE SERVICE OF SEVERAL WOMEN

Throughout the New Testament there are many women mentioned and noted for their unique service for the kingdom of God. In our discussion, I will limit myself to some of the women Paul mentions in his letters.

EUODIA AND SYNTYCHE

In the first place let us look at the service provided by Euodia and Syntyche, mentioned in Paul's letter to the Philippians (4:2). On the one hand, the apostle admonishes the women to be of "the same mind in the Lord" and not to quarrel. On the other hand, however, Paul praises these women because "they have contended at my side in the cause of the gospel" (vs. 3). Specifically, what these women did is not mentioned. From his comments, however, it is clear that these were influential women in the church of Philippi, and that they had provided the church there with valuable services.

The special service of women here was not strange. In Acts 16 we read that Paul and Silas had first preached the gospel to a group of women. This was the first city the apostles visited in Europe and the Word of God had laid claim on the hearts of women. About Lydia, the dealer in purple goods, Luke expressly writes that "the Lord opened her heart to respond to Paul's message" (vs. 14). In Philippi, women were the first among the congregation, and therefore it is not surprising they zealously worked to effectuate the impact of God's Word. In this latter context, Paul mentions that Euodia and Syntyche worked beside Clement and other workers to promote the cause of the gospel. He urges them to assist these women.

No doubt, his words were not only to promote the restoration of the relationship between Euodia and Syntyche, but also to encourage the congregation to work together with them to promote the gospel.

These women had been called to a lofty service in God's kingdom, to help the church spread God's Word, the preaching of the gospel, the message of salvation!

PHOEBE

In the conclusion to his letter to the Romans, Paul mentions several women, first of all, Phoebe. He calls her "our sister Phoebe, a deacon, of the church in Cenchreae" (16:1). The apostle requests that they "receive her in the Lord in a way worthy of his people and to give her any help she may need from you" (vs. 2). The church is encouraged to assist her if she needs assistance. Why? Paul states, "for she has been the benefactor of many people, including me" (vs. 2). Some people suggest that Phoebe had actually delivered his letter to the church at Rome when Paul was still in Corinth. She is introduced as "a deacon of the church in Cenchreae" the harbour city that lay to the east of Corinth. Based on the term, "deacon", some exegetes also maintain that she was officially ordained as deacon in the church. The word here actually means "servant." Therefore, its use is too ambiguous to be able to conclude that she was officially a deacon. Her service can also refer to various forms of help she offered, protection or hospitality. From Paul's request we can conclude that Phoebe assisted many people in Cenchreae, including Paul himself. She seems to have been a woman of means, so she was able to help others. If we consider the fact that Cenchreae was a busy harbour, then it would make sense that there were frequent travellers that needed help: shelter, or advice and support. Paul had experienced that help himself. Therefore, Phoebe is mentioned as an honourable woman who used her gifts and talents for the promotion of God's kingdom.

PRISCILLA

In Romans 16:3, Paul mentions Priscilla, the wife of Aquila. Isn't it rather remarkable that he mentions her name before he mentions her husband? He also does that in his letter to Timothy, and Luke does the same in his writing of Acts.

Although Paul occasionally reverses the order (e.g., 1 Cor. 16:19), it is important to note that normally Priscilla is mentioned first. Especially, in those days, that order is not unimportant. And surely, it was not Paul's intention to make Priscilla the head of their family. Therefore, we must conclude that Priscilla, in her zeal and effort on behalf of the church of Jesus Christ, shone with distinction. This couple meant a lot for several congregations. In Corinth they provided Paul with a place to live and a livelihood. In Ephesus, apparently anointed by the Holy Spirit, and full of the Spirit, they assisted a special office-bearer, Apollos, to come to a clearer understanding concerning the gospel of Jesus Christ. Together, they used their knowledge and gifts to instruct Apollos.

In Rome, this couple received the congregation in their house, and served the Lord Christ in such a committed manner that Paul calls them his co-workers. While still in Corinth himself, the apostle writes the congregation in Rome that Prisca (Priscilla) and Aquila had risked their lives for Paul and adds, "Not only I but all the churches of the Gentiles are grateful to them" (16:3). Later, when the apostle is awaiting his trial in Rome, he again mentioned the names of this couple.

Priscilla especially, must have really excelled in her dedication and service. Clearly, when Paul writes about this, it has nothing to do with overthrowing established cultural expectations, or a form of early feminism, as if he shortchanges the honour that is normally due to men. On the contrary, the apostle wants his readers to know about the impact of god-fearing women. In the face of cultural norms, he dares to put her in the first place because she gave so much for God's church, and as woman, even dared to risk her life for God's apostle.

OTHER WOMEN

In Romans 16, Paul mentions several other women. A certain Mary in Rome is given a special greeting, and she is praised for the special effort she made on behalf of the congregation in Rome. Tryphena and Tryphosa are mentioned separately at the end of the letter: "those women who work hard in the Lord." Similarly, he says, "Greet my dear friend Persis, another woman who has worked very hard in the Lord." These women, in all likelihood, had dedicated themselves in looking after the needs of the believers.

There are an additional number of women he mentions without more elaboration: the mother of Rufus, Julia, and the sister of Nereus. One thing is clear, in the midst of a world where women were not reckoned or esteemed, even disdained, women are named who had an important role in the spread of the gospel.

Paul's recognition of these women does not mean that they carried out official work as ordained deacons/elders. But it is quite clear that in the churches in Paul's day, women provided a wide variety of services. Additionally, it is clear that the services that the apostle praised, went far beyond volunteering to nurse the sick or other forms of mercy. The sisters had been engaged in the spread of God's Word. They confessed God's name and they dared to show their commitment. For the sake of the gospel, they presented themselves as a holy sacrifice in service to the church of Christ. They joined the struggle against sin, the devil. In short, they devoted themselves with the dedication of their whole life, in the struggle for God's kingdom.

7. A Contradiction in the Bible?

Prophesize or remain silent?

There are more letters Paul wrote which deserve special attention with respect to the service of women in the church. In both 1 Cor. 11 and 1 Cor. 14, the apostle addresses the role of women.

In the first reference above, Paul says, "But every woman who prays or prophesies with her head uncovered dishonors her head—it is the same as having her head shaved" (1 Cor. 11:5). In 1 Cor. 14:34, he states, "Women should remain silent in the churches. They are not allowed to speak, but must be in submission, as the law says." Both of the above Bible texts have raised a number of questions.

In the first place, when he writes about the congregation of Corinth, does the apostle Paul refer to situations in the *gathering* of the church or congregation? In the second place, what does the apostle mean when he says the women should *remain silent* in the congregation? Is the apostle imposing an absolute silence on women?

If both questions must be answered affirmatively, are we not confronted with a contradiction here? On the one side women prophesize, but on the other they are to remain silent. In other words, is it possible to find agreement between 1 Cor. 11:5 and 1 Cor. 14:34?

Let's first establish the fact that the Holy Scriptures do not contradict themselves, and similarly, that the apostle Paul, led by the Holy Spirit does not contradict himself either.

It is clear that prophecy, also in the New Testament, served to edify the congregation. The apostle stresses that. But that appears to mean that the impression is given that this prophesying took place in the midst of the congregation. The apostle says in chapter 11, "Every man who prays or prophesies with his head covered dishonors his head. But every woman who prays or prophesies with her head uncovered dishonors her head—it is the same as having her head shaved." From this text it also appears that Paul is referring to the gathering of the congregation because it was not necessary for women to cover their heads in the privacy of their homes. Where would she prophesy other than in the midst of the congregation? Exegetes admit that without the cross reference to 1 Cor. 14, everyone would be led to conclude that we must think of prophesying in a public gathering.

If we answer the first question affirmatively, and conclude that in 1 Cor. 11 the apostle is speaking of a public gathering, then how must we make that fit appropriately with 1 Cor. 14:34? Is the latter injunction, women must remain silent, an absolute? Some people have embraced that position. Such an absolute becomes problematic in the light of 1 Cor. 11:5 where we read that women were permitted to pray and prophesy, albeit in a limited fashion (i.e., keeping their position as woman in mind).

In 1 Cor. 14 Paul is writing specifically about married women, as verse 35 indicates: "If they want to inquire about something, they should ask their own husbands at home." One should not suggest that Paul could also mean brother, brother-in-law, uncle, etc., because the words *at home* and *their own husbands* clearly refer to a married woman. Concerning these married women, the apostle says that they, "must be in submission" (vs. 34). He uses the same word in Ephesians 5 when he refers to the marriage relationship. For the sake of Christ, she must recognize her husband as her head. It is to that submission to their husbands that Paul also refers to here in 1 Cor. 14:35. In other words, his comments do not concern an absolute prohibition of women prophesying. But married women should not mistake their being married by trying to take the place of the man (i.e., their husband).

Paul wants to prevent confusion and chaos in the congregation. The one should not interrupt the other; they must accommodate each other. But concerning the married women, there is another stipulation: she must step back to accommodate her husband's headship. When Paul states that women in the congregation should remain quiet, the character of that restraint is explained: "They are not allowed to speak, but must be in submission, as the law says" (1 Cor. 14:34). The apostle applies this injunction to the marriage relationship. For the Greek word *speaking*, the apostle uses another word than prophesying. *At home*, the women are expected to ask for clarification. Apparently, this 'asking' concerned women who posed questions for the sake of clarification, initiating a discussion. These women, according to Paul, forget their proper position as female spouse. Understanding the words in this way, takes away the apparent contradiction between 1 Cor. 11:5 and 1 Cor. 14:34.

When we read about *prophesying* we should think of the charismatic gifts that Paul mentions in his letter, specifically, the gift of prophesying. He states, "There are different kinds of gifts, but the same Spirit distributes them" (1 Cor. 12:4), urging them, "Now eagerly desire the greater gifts" (1 Cor. 12:31). In conclusion, Paul points to the ultimate way: "Now eagerly desire the greater gifts" (1 Cor. 12:31) and then writes his well-known chapter about love, (1 Corinthians 13), in which he describes the perfect form of service.

A LONGING FOR EMANCIPATION IN CORINTH

When we look closely at the context of life in Corinth, a few things become clearer. Earlier, I spoke about *hetaira*[1] (escorts/prostitutes) in Greece. Though these women were public women (prostitutes) they were often quite sophisticated, often functioned as escorts for famous Greeks, and attended special festivities as dancers or musicians. Many put on airs of sophistication, participated in philosophic discussions, and engaged in public debate with men. No doubt, they remained very well aware of the subordinate position that most women had in Greece. As such, the *hetaira* exemplified a form of early women's emancipation.

If you picture congregational life in Greece against this light, the apparent contradiction between 1 Cor. 11:5 and 1 Cor. 14:34 disappears. From what Paul writes, it seems that women in the Corinthian church wanted to reason and criticize, debate and argue, as the *hetaera* were accustomed to do. At that point, the apostle says, no, because that is abuse of the liberty that the Lord God had given women, a misuse of freedom in Christ, and also a misuse of free speech that was unique to the congregation of Christ, a gift in Christ's congregation that was given in the *charismata* of the Holy Spirit.

The apostle passionately opposed this misdirected hankering for emancipation. Women who love Christ, Paul teaches, must avoid this spirit of false liberty. If a

---

1. Hetaira, (Greek: "female companion") Latin hetaera, one of a class of professional independent courtesans of ancient Greece who, besides developing physical beauty, cultivated their minds and talents to a degree far beyond that allowed to the average Attic woman. Usually living fashionably alone, or sometimes two or three together, the hetairai enjoyed an enviable and respected position of wealth and were protected and taxed by the state. Though they were generally foreigners, slaves, or freedwomen, their freedom was greater than that of the married woman, who was bound to seclusion. That their homes were frequented by married men was not censured by society. (Encyclopedia Britannica online.)

woman has questions about the word that was spoken in the congregation, let her remain silent and ask her husband for clarification at home.

In 1 Cor. 14, Paul asks the congregation: when such women push their own agenda what kind of an impression will such women make on outsiders? "It is disgraceful for a woman to speak in the church" (14:35). This latter comment is clearly aligned with 1 Cor. 11 where the apostle addresses this matter: "it is a disgrace for a woman to have her hair cut off or her head shaved, (vs. 6) . . . if a woman has long hair, it is her glory" (vs. 15). By cutting her hair, a woman discards her worthiness, and therefore, Paul declares, her head must be covered or she should be veiled. The woman bears her authority (literally in Greek: her authority,) on her head. Her licence to pray and to prophesy is never to be separated from her subordination to her husband. Only with her covered head, in her qualification as wife, is she actually empowered. In this way, she bears her authority on her head.

The apostle even mentions the angels in this context because the angels are constantly concerned about the well-being of the church. They are sent out on behalf of those who will receive salvation. Elsewhere in Scripture, we read that angels are eager to know about God's plan of salvation. They are charged to be on watch for the congregation. Therefore, it is not just people that we must be concerned about and whose opinion we must be aware of, but there is more. There are multitudes of angels, many thousands who are aware of paradise, and have had an important role in the history of salvation with regard to the salvation of God's people.

Therefore, there is no place for a hankering for emancipation in God's congregation. Men and women have to acknowledge their proper place. Men must provide leadership, however. The apostle places special emphasis on this – this does not detract from the equivalence of men and women "for as woman came from man, so also man is born of woman. But everything comes from God" (1 Cor. 11:12). He is the Source and the Origin of everything, of all creatures, and therefore, also of both men and women!

Witch ducking. - During the Middle Ages and into the 16th and 17th centuries, it was assumed that water was pure and reject the impure witch. Therefore, a witch would float. If the woman sank, she was not a witch.

8. OTHER DEVELOPMENTS TO THE ROLE OF WOMEN

PROPHETESSES

What happened subsequently to the role and position of women in the church in the wake of the apostolic period? It has been established that during the early Christian church, women were integrally involved in reaching out with God's Word. This particular role was perhaps unique because men were forbidden access to women's quarters. There are a number of extant apostolic references and apostolic traditions that indicate that women, especially leading women of the day, had a significant role. The synagogues remained as important places where these connections were made, especially with proselytes. Apparently in that latter group, women were in the majority. Via these women, the Word of God was proclaimed in the imperial courts. Some even claim that Poppaea Sabina[1], wife of the cruel emperor Nero (54 – 68 A.D.), was one of these god-fearing women. The claim is also made that because of her, the first persecution of Christians took place. Celsus[2], one of the most fanatic opponents of the church, stated that among those converted to Christianity were many leading Christian women. This was at a time that Christian men were a rare occurrence in the ruling class. Pomponia Graecina (died 83 A.D.), wife of the proconsul Aulus Plautius, was one of the first leading women publicly accused of being a Christian.

---

1. Poppaea Sabina (30 - 65 A.D.)–known as Poppaea Sabina the Younger. Most writers of the period (Tacitus, Cassius Dio, Suetonius) were very critical of Poppaea Sabina, describing her as a very self-serving person. Only the Jewish historian Josephus is complimentary.

2. Celsus - 2nd century Greek philosopher, wrote critically of Christianity. The Church Father, Origen of Alexandria, vigorously defended Christianity over against him.

During the reign of Emperor Commodus (180-192 A.D.), there were many Christians in the imperial court. Among them there was a certain Marcia, known for her influence among the courtiers and her work on behalf of her co-religionists. Among Commodus' successor (Emperor Perinax, (192-193 A.D.) there were also many Christians at the court.

Toward the end of the first century there was also a prophetess in Thyatira. We may assume that at the time that the book of Revelation of John was written, a certain Jezebel (either her real name or one given symbolically) was active in the congregation. Revelation 2:20-23 tells us that she had a bad influence there. If the translation "your wife" is correct (2:20) (and we have no reason not to accept this) then she was the wife of the local pastor. Jezebel promoted a prophecy of "accommodation" with the pagan culture. Therefore, Christ warns his congregation to reject this accommodation theory and he goes so far as to call this misleading prophecy "adultery" (vs. 22) similar to how the unrepentant church in Revelation is presented in contrast to his congregation as the heavenly queen.

A few years after the death of the apostle John, Justin Martyr[3] said, "Among us men and women are found who have received gifts of grace from the Holy Spirit." During this same century, the Church Father, Irenaeus[4] stated that prophesying by both men and women should be maintained and encouraged in the church. During his ministry, prophetesses still functioned in the church. At the end of this century, however, prophecy diminished and eventually disappeared. Institutionalized liturgy eventually took the place of the charismata.[5]

OTHER EXAMPLES OF MINISTRIES BY WOMEN

There were other women ministries in the early Christian church that endured beyond this period, especially the diaconate (deaconesses) and ministry of widows[6] (cf. 1 Timothy 5:3-16). Around 112 A.D., the governor of Bithynia, Pliny

---

3. Justin Martyr (died 165 A.D.) was an early Christian apologist.

4. Irenaeus (c. 130 - 202 A.D.) was Greek theologian and apologist, later bishop of Lyons, France.

5. Charismata (pl.) charism (s.) - supernatural grace, unique power that some people received from the Holy Spirit for the benefit of others, especially during the early church period: prophesying, miraculous healing (e.g., by laying on hands), speaking in tongues. In 1 Cor. 12:8-10 the apostle Paul provides a list of such charismata.
In the Reformed churches it is generally assumed that some of these more miraculous gifts (prophesying, miraculous healing, speaking in tongues) was time-bound, limited to the early period of the church. With the advent of the complete New Testament canon and the stable growth of the church, it is assumed that the church no longer needed these supernatural gifts. Remember, however, that the acquisition of faith and regeneration are in themselves miraculous gifts of the Holy Spirit, as emphasized by the Canons of Dort. Pentecostal churches and charismatic movements within other churches maintain that the presence of charismatic gifts today, is evidence of a living church. They ascribe unique powers to people who receive these special charismata by means of prayers and contemplation.

6. 1 Timothy 5:3-16. Paul provides Timothy with advice concerning widows. Younger widows were to re-marry, but older widows could serve in a diaconal ministry.

the Younger (61-113 A.D.) wrote to the Emperor Trajan in Rome, "By means of torture I tried to extract the truth from two maidens who were called *'ministrae'* (servants/deacons) about the rumours concerning Christians." These women were called "servants" and from this it is assumed that they were deaconesses.

About a century later, the term 'deaconess' again arises in the Eastern church and specifically, in the Syriac *'Didaskalia Apostolorum'* [7] (The Teaching or Instruction of the Apostles) written in the third century. In this document, the services of deaconesses are claimed to be an essential ministry in the church. These deaconesses worked together with male deacons. In the worship services, however, they were not deemed to be of equal importance with the deacons. In the non-liturgical activities, they were equally esteemed. They maintained contact between the bishop and other women, ministered to the sick and those recovering from illnesses; they did work "that was inappropriate for men."

Deaconesses were also allowed to *assist* in the baptism of women, who were often partly undressed and were baptized either by immersion or affusion.[8] They looked after the anointing with oil, though they were not allowed to administer anointing of the head, and perform the actual administration of baptism.[9] These latter rituals could only be administered by the bishop, a presbyter (elder), or a deacon. In addition to the above ministries, women also continued to fulfill an important role in the Order or Class of Widows, also called the *"viduat"*.[10] Further evidence

---

7. The Didaskalia Apostolorum, written in the third century (ca. 230 AD). The leadership of the early Christian church claimed that it was written by the apostles at the Council of Jerusalem. Contemporary scholars assert that this document has its origin around 230 AD and served as an instruction for the churches.

8. Affusion – pouring water over the head from a bowl.

9. The anointing (of the head) with oil, and baptism were both deemed to be sacraments.

10. "An intermediate position between office and congregation is occupied by the "class of widows" (1 Tim. 5: 3-16) while in the general ethics of the N.T. times the widows stand at the lower level on the social scale and along with orphans, are the object of special care (James 1: 27, Acts 6: 1ff.). The Pastoral Letters in contrast for the first time presuppose the existence of a class of widows in the congregational life that plays a special role (Viduat). This group is frequently documented in the later church. A distinction is also made between older and younger widows. The latter group are to marry, bear children and manage the household and thus should not rely on the support of the church. The older widows (>60 years) who have been married to only one husband and have a good reputation in other respects may be entered into the official list of widows (1 Tim. 5: 9-10)." Theology of the New Testament. by Georg Strecker – Copyright 1996 Walter de Gruyter & Co., Berlin. P. 178 ff.
M. Cathleen Kaveny: The Order of Widows: What the Early Church can Teach us about Older Women and Health Care –
"At the root of the Hebrew word for widow, almanah is the word alem, which means "unable to speak" (Thurston, 1989 Thurston, B. B. 1989. The widows: A woman's ministry in the early Church, Minneapolis: Fortress Press. [Google Scholar], p. 9). In the social framework of biblical Judaism, as in many other Near Eastern societies of that time, women could not speak for themselves; they were dependent upon the care and protection of male relatives who had legal authority to speak on their behalf. An adult woman's social status and security was determined by her roles as wife, mother, and mistress of the household; her husband was responsible for supporting her and representing her in all matters of public concern. Consequently, the death of a husband meant not only personal grief, but also radical social upheaval and economic uncertainty. As the widowed Naomi's lament to her daughter-in-law Ruth demonstrates, it was a fate most feared and bemoaned by women."
Cathleen Kaveny adds, "Widows made house visitations, where they comforted, fasted, and prayed with the sick and gave practical instruction to younger women. They prophesied. Enrolled widows also assumed a place of honor in the liturgy, sitting in the front of the assembly along with the bishops, priests, and deacons."
See: https://www.tandfonline.com/doi/full/10.1080/13803600590926369

of this is provided by Ignatius, Bishop of Antioch[11] (a contemporary of Polycarp) who addressed the women who were listed as widows. The latter formed a separate group called the *"viduat"*, which apparently also included unmarried women. Along with Polycarp of Smyrna, these women were called an "altar of God" who were expected to be involved in matters of faith, in prayer and good deeds. Another source relates that these widows visited a certain Peregrinus when he was imprisoned.

In the third century our sources indicate that this order of widows had special duties: continuing prayer for the whole church, fasting for the sick, laying on hands on the sick and other ministries of charity. It was determined that these widows were placed under the supervision of the bishop, the presbyters and the deacons, and that they were not allowed to be involved in teaching about difficult religious issues. They were not permitted to do home visits on their own, or catechise.

Another important source of information is called the *Constitutiones Apostolorum*.[12] The *Constitutiones* indicate that the *viduat* was still functional in the fourth century, but not in the midst of the congregation. These women were expected to serve God by singing psalms, praying and fasting. In the congregation, the *viduat* or Order of Widows appears to have been completely displaced by deaconesses. These women were deemed to be more highly esteemed and were chosen from a separate group or class of women. Only if a young woman was unavailable, could a widow serve in this capacity.

The ministry of the deaconesses had been substantially expanded: assisting with baptism, care of the sick, accompanying women who visited the bishop. Basically, all the special care of women in the congregation became the task of the deaconesses, a role which even included a form of ushering for women (i.e., showing women (also guest women) their place in worship).

Changes

During the latter part of the fourth century there were many liturgical changes, as the church hierarchy became more established. An increasing number of people attended worship because persecutions had come to an end (with Emperor Constantine), and as the church gradually transitioned to become a state church.

---

11. Ignatius was martyred in Rome, around 140 A.D.

12. The Apostolic Constitutions or Constitutions of the Holy Apostles, compiled around 375-380 A.D., is a Christian collection of eight treatises which belongs to the Church Orders, a genre of early Christian literature, that offered authoritative "apostolic" prescriptions on moral conduct, liturgy and Church organization. The first part is a re-written Didaskalia. As the title suggests, the claim was made that this document was also an instruction from the apostles.

The role of women in worship decreased, and instead, men and women were increasingly segregated during the liturgical procedures.

Bishop Cyril[13] of Jerusalem introduced the practice of catechism instruction for baptized members before Easter and liturgical exorcisms. During this latter rite, men were expected to sit with men, and women with the women. As they waited, one man had to read to another. "If there is no book available," Cyril stated, "the one can pray and others can engage in an appropriate discussion." There had to be a clear distinction between men and women. In keeping with Cyril's reading of 1 Cor. 14:34 and 1 Tim. 2:12, he forbade women to read as they awaited the exorcism. They were allowed to sit together, sing psalms or read in silence. Though their lips were allowed to move, no sound was permitted.

All the rites of anointing, baptism, and eucharist were discussed by Cyril, and in many places, he pointed to the ministry of the bishop, presbyters, and deacons. Women were not even mentioned. Apparently, the deacons had become the assistants of the bishops, as these men became more and more dominant in the church liturgy. For example, men and women, when they participated in the veneration of the cross on Good Friday, were expected not only to kiss the wood of the cross, but also kiss the hand of the bishop.
In this period, *nuns* began to assume more significant roles. A wealthy woman named Egeria[14], travelled on a pilgrimage from a cloister in Aquitaine (on the border of France and Spain) to the East. She stayed in Jerusalem for a considerable time and described, among other things, how nuns attended services in the holy sites.

In the writings of a contemporary of Cyril, John Chrysostom[15], the deaconess is still mentioned. Though he is aware of the *viduat,* clearly it no longer functions in his time. In the 5th century, deaconesses are mentioned as the "keepers of the holy doors". In the 6th century they still appear to have a church function.

In many places the role of deaconesses steadily eroded. By the end of the 4th century, they were not functioning anymore in Jerusalem, and around 394 A.D., the Synod of Nîmes (France) forbade the use of deaconesses. In the East, in Byzantium, however, deaconesses were employed into the 11th century. This 'office' disappeared entirely in the West, as the Council of Orange (441 A.D.) and the Councils of Epaone (517 A.D.) and Orléans (511 A.D.) forbade the ordination of

---

13. Bishop Cyril (Cyrillus) of Jerusalem (313 - 386 A.D.)

14. Egeria wrote an account of her travels to Jerusalem (ca. 380). The beginning and the end of her account is lost. The booklet provides interesting linguistic information about the development of vulgar Latin, and about various practices during her time.

15. John Chrysostom (349- 407 A.D.), archbishop of Constantinople. A prolific writer, gifted preacher.

deaconesses. At the latter council[16], women were officially excluded because of the "frailty" of their gender, and at the second Synod of Maçon (581 A.D.) a discussion was generated by one of the bishops who maintained that women cannot be called humans. According to the Council of Auxerre, women were not allowed to touch the bread of the eucharist with bare hands because they would defile it.

MIDDLE AGES

The status of women in the church (and society!) continued to deteriorate during the Middle Ages, also because of the authoritative position given to the theology of Thomas Aquinas[17] (1225 – 1275 AD). In many respects he considered women to be inferior to men. The man, according to Thomas, is the primary purpose of the woman; he is considered to be normative. The woman, however, is deemed to be 'deficient and faulty', a creature of lesser intellect compared to men. Only a baptized man was allowed to participate in the sacrament of consecration. This view taught by Thomas Aquinas had a tremendous impact on the Roman Catholic church. Consequently, women almost completely disappeared from the practice of congregational life. The ideal woman, the model woman, disappeared behind the protective and confining walls of a cloister; abbesses and nuns completely replaced the ministry of deaconesses.

Another threat to women appeared in the late Middle Ages: accusations of witchcraft and witch hunts became more prevalent. More often than not, the focus of this superstition was directed at women who were accused of black magic arts. Thousands were maliciously tortured and burned. In the small city of Wiesensteig, for example, a community of several hundred people, 63 women were burned in one year! Papal inquisitors published a booklet toward the end of the 15th century, called the *Hammer of the Witches*.[18] In a view endorsed by the pope, the writer, Heinich Kramer, maintained that he had discovered a new conspiracy, asserting that principally women had covenanted with the devil, had sexual intercourse with him and even had generated children through this relationship. Men, on the other hand, were made impotent by their magic spells. Because men believed

---

16. With collapse of the Roman Empire, the face of European society changed radically as Germanic tribes took over control of the countryside. Eventually, the Germanic people also controlled affairs in the church. That meant that they imposed their ethnic views and attitudes toward women on the church. Until the Reformation, women were often deemed to be little more than chattels with few rights and of little value. Holy orders and the refuge of cloisters were usually their only reprieve. In fact, daughters were deemed to be a financial burden and therefore the monastery was often a cheap way to accommodate a daughter's future needs.

17. Thomas Aquinas - (1225 - 1274 AD), was an immensely important figure in the Medieval church: Dominican monk, priest, philosopher, teacher, writer, etc. He wrote a standard theological "text" called the Summa Theologiae that became the authoritative view of the Roman Catholic church. The R.C. church calls him a Doctor of the Church.

18. Maleus Maleficarum (1487 AD). by Heinrich Kramer (a discredited clergyman). The faculty of the University of Cologne condemned the book as unethical and in contravention to Roman Catholic canon law.

that women had a defective intellect, they were far more inclined than men, to fall away from the faith. Their evil vengeance would know no bounds if someone had offended them. For many years this terrible superstition fueled the hatred of European society against many women whose worst offence was perhaps being in the wrong place at the wrong time.

Reformation

The Great Reformation of the 16th century also meant reformation with respect to the attitudes and views toward women and women's ministry in the church of Christ. Frequently, Luther preached about women in the Bible to prove that women should show leadership when men fail to step up to their responsibility. "If it happens," he said in a sermon dated 1522, "that there is no man present, then a woman can step up and preach to others as best as she can."

In several church orders at that time, it was recommended to retain women to minister to the sick and serve as midwives. They were to be instructed by the minister concerning the spiritual aspect of their work. Sometimes they were called "church ministries" and were reimbursed by the diaconate.

From the outset, Calvin recognized that the care of the needy is a responsibility of the church and wanted to engage women in the congregation for this task. He was of the opinion that women were not to be admitted to a "public office", with the exception of the diaconate. He made a distinction between two types of deacon: the one group is responsible for the financially needy (alms), and the other group, engaging the women, who were to look after the sick.

Calvin's thinking was subsequently adopted in the articles of Wesel (1568). The actual practice of a woman's diaconate, however, did not last long in the Reformed churches in the Netherlands. Regardless of critical synod decisions, there were local churches that incorporated deaconesses, a few lasted into the 17th century. The prominent Dutch theologian Voetius[19] was in favour of establishing the services of deaconesses but he did not want to see deaconesses recognized as a separate office, but rather, as assistants to the deacons.

Actually, some of Voetius' comments about women could lead us to question whether this leading Calvinist thinker considered women to be totally human, and whether they were created in the image of God. Other theologians also maintained that women were inferior to men and were totally subordinate to men.

---

19. Gijsbertus Voetius (1589-1676), Dutch Calvinist theologian. He was the youngest delegate at the Synod of Dort (1618/19). In 1634 he was appointed professor of theology at the University of Utrecht.

Deformation and then . . .

In the 18th century, women in the church and society were relegated to a non-active or passive role. The rise of a dualistic morality also became prevalent, well into the 19th century. Many leaders embraced a double standard: men appeared to be allowed to engage in all kinds of immorality, but women or young ladies had to bear the brunt of the blame and were forced to shoulder the disrepute that resulted from cases of sexual misadventures.

In the Reformed churches in the Netherlands, several leaders, however, initiated a significant change in attitudes toward women. Rev. Ottho Gerard Heldring (1804 – 1876) established a home for former prostitutes and established other philanthropic institutions.[20]

Rev. L. Lindeboom[21] is recognized for the special efforts that he made to re-engage the service of women in the church. He posed the question, "Is it not remarkable that of all the people who were miraculously healed, that it was a leading woman whom the apostles raised from the dead? Through this miraculous event, did the LORD not provide a clear sign in the congregation of the Lord that the work of women is vital?"

Dr. Abraham Kuyper[22] appeared on the ecclesiastical scene as one of the leaders of the Second Secession[23] (1886). Kuyper encouraged also the women to acknowledge their calling to choose the one Sovereign, Jesus Christ, in the struggles in the church. He also appealed to society at large (i.e., the male voters) of his day to allow women to have a voice in politics, to allow them to vote in elections.

On the flipside

Attitudes toward women and their role in both church affairs and in society often ran parallel courses. Reformers in the church reached out to change attitudes toward the active engagement of women.

---

20. In Germany and England there were also religious revivals. In England, for example, John Wesley, Geo. Whitefield and others called the people back to the Bible, also in their attitudes toward women.

21. Dr. Lucas Lindeboom (1845-1933), Dutch Reformed minister and professor at the Theological Seminary in Kampen.

22. Dr. Abraham Kuyper (1837-1920), Dutch Calvinist theologian. A leader of the Second Secession (Doleantie) in 1886, leader of the Anti-Revolutionary Party, Prime Minister of the Netherlands, professor, philosopher at the Free University, Amsterdam. In many Western countries it was not until well into the 20th century that women were allowed to vote in civic and national elections.

23. During the Second Secession (Doleantie), led especially by Dr. Kuyper, many more people left the state church in protest against its increasing liberalism and progressivism. In 1892, members of the First Secession (1834) and those of the Second Secession joined to form the Reformed Churches of the Netherlands.

In society, however, other and new philosophic forces were at work, most notably, the revolutionary principles of the French Revolution: liberty, equality and fraternity. One could call these principles a "cri de coeur" of Western society to liberate women from the shackles of past oppression, a drive to liberate or emancipate women. During the 20th century, this movement would pick up tremendous energy and grow in popularity. Equality would mean many different things: women had to embrace self-determination in the home, in society, and eventually self-determination in matters of their fertility. The roles of father and mother should be interchangeable for men and women.

In the name of equality and liberation, women demanded total equality with men in whatever role or position they chose. Was it surprising then, that this equality was also demanded in religious matters? Especially in Protestant churches questions were raised about why women were excluded from the offices of the church. Many people claimed that freedom in the kingdom meant that women should be allowed to teach, lead in worship and lead in church affairs. These critics asserted with emphasis that churches in the Western world had actually understood very little of the gospel message. Also, in the Roman Catholic church progressive voices increasingly demanded an equal voice for women and the admission of women into the priesthood.

In the World Council of Churches[24], almost at the outset (1948), delegates insisted that women should be granted equality with men in all offices and roles.

The demand to admit women to all the offices of the church is no longer limited to the 'progressives' in liberal churches. Also, in Reformed churches the demand to admit women to all the offices has become more prevalent. In this context, I must emphasize that there is an essential difference between revolutionary demand for equality as the spirit of contemporary opinion expresses this, and the Reformed views that are rooted in the Scriptures. There is a difference between unscriptural emancipation and Scriptural reformation!

---

24. World Council of Churches (WCC) was established in Amsterdam in 1948 as a post-World War II ecumenical movement. The WCC now includes representation of most mainline Protestant churches, Orthodox Eastern, Assyrian, Moravian, Methodist, Mennonite, etc. churches. Note: the Roman Catholic church (though it sends observers) is not a member, nor are conservative and more orthodox churches. The WCC seeks ecumenical unity above differences in religious views.

9. Women in the Ruling Offices of the Church?

Not Permitted

"I believe that women should be permitted to become office-bearers." That statement could be heard with increasing frequency in many 'progressive' churches in the last generations. Though women have become prevalent in ruling offices in many church denominations,[1] the Liberated Reformed Churches[2] (GKv) resisted pressure to accede to this change.[3]

There was, however, another issue that continued to spur discussion: Should communicant women be permitted to vote for office-bearers? In the Netherlands, this

---

1. The Christian Reformed Church, after three decades of discussion and debate, decided at their 1995 Synod to admit women to the ruling offices of the church. By 2018, at least 25% of the churches still did not have women in leadership positions. Women graduates from their seminary complained that they had to wait much longer than men to receive a call. The 1995 decision prompted many people to leave the CRC, leading, among others, to the formation of the United Reformed Churches in North America.

2. The Reformed Churches, (Liberated), (GKv) came into being in 1944 after the General Synod of the Reformed Churches deposed Dr. K. Schilder, Dr. S. Greijdanus and others because they would not subscribe to synodical decisions concerning their adopted views of the covenant that had been promoted by Dr. A. Kuyper and his followers. Up to 1944, the interpretation or acceptance of Kuyper's views were left in the freedom of the churches. The General Synod of Sneek changed that and forced all ministers and office-bearers to embrace the views endorsed by the synod.

3. Several recent General Synods of Liberated Reformed Churches in the Netherlands (GKv) discussed the role of women in the church, especially with a view to admitting them to the ruling offices. At their synod in 2017, it was decided to admit women to all the ruling offices of the church. Churches were given the freedom to implement this decision, or not. Many churches have already (2019) moved forward and appointed women as elders, deacons and ministers. At the General Synod of Meppel, the decision was based on a new hermeneutical interpretation of several Bible texts (1 Cor. 14: 34, and 1 Tim. 2: 12) In short, the claim was made that the texts that forbade women to rule or teach in the church were time-bound and culturally unacceptable in the context of the 21st century. This decision had to bring the GKv in line with the Dutch cultural expectations with respect to the roles of women. In the wake of this decision, the GKv were expelled from the International Conference of Reformed Churches and many member churches discontinued their ecclesiastical fellowship with the GKv.

issue had been discussed at several Reformed synods since the 1930s. We'll come back to this issue in the next chapter.

Admission

In 1954, the synod of the largest Reformed denomination in the Netherlands decided to admit women into the ruling offices. Similar to the Christian Reformed Church of North America (see footnote 1, Pg. 65), the orthodox/conservative 'wing' in this Dutch church was very unhappy about this decision. They were convinced that 1 Cor. 14:34, and 1 Tim. 2:12 clearly forbade women to teach or rule in the church. Several interesting statements were made in regards to reaching the synod decision:

> The emancipation of women cannot be compared to the prohibition of slavery. God did not create free and slave people, but he created people in his image, as men and women.
>
> The prohibition against women in 1 Cor. 14:34 is related to discussions at meetings of the congregation. This includes exclusion of women from the office of minister.
>
> The prohibition against women in 1 Cor. 14:34 concerned married women. It does not track what Paul allows young (unmarried) women and widows to do, but forbids married women.
>
> In 1 Tim. 2:12 women are denied the right to admonish the congregation; it follows logically that the preaching of the gospel would certainly be forbidden.
>
> The prohibition prescribed by Paul, includes both the unmarried and the married women.
>
> The widows mentioned in 1 Tim. 2:12 do not have a leadership office similar to the older women mentioned in Titus 2:3.
>
> After the Reformation in the Netherlands, deaconesses were appointed in several places, but this was not made into an official office.

Time-bound?

One more important statement was made that opposed the admission of women into the ruling offices:
The historical context of Paul's injunction in 1 Cor. 14: 34 was neither time-bound nor situational; in Corinth women wanted more influence and power. Otherwise the prohibition stated by Paul would have been unnecessary.
The issue whether this prohibition is *time-bound* has become a major contention in the discussions about the role of women in the church. Another Reformed

denomination in the Netherlands, the so-called synodical Reformed Church[4], gradually moved from a traditional prohibition (1948) to a more nuanced view (1954) that incorporated a positive consideration of contemporary customs and mores. It was acknowledged that Paul had forbidden women to teach or rule, but the theologians nuanced this exclusive position by suggesting that God had not created this order in the beginning. They generate the perception that the apostle Paul had not progressed any farther in his thinking than his Jewish-rabbinical tradition in which he was brought up.

This matter is not incidental to this discussion; it is fundamental. The proponents of change in the synodical Reformed Church admit that they changed their hermeneutical[5] thinking. They add that this change serves to undergird this shift of view. In 1965, the above Reformed denomination took the next step and admitted women into the ruling offices.[6] The theologians claim that these new insights into Scripture have not weakened Scripture, but instead, the understanding of Scriptures has been clarified. On the opposite side of the argument, however, critics respond that if the norms and values of Scripture are no longer accepted, then the new interpretation and exegesis will be skewed to its real and intended meaning.

In actual fact, the agents of change push the argument of "time-bound" Bible references to the point that they put words in the apostle's mouth and have him declare things he never said. Clearly, this form of Bible hermeneutics creates a very slippery slope: the normative character of the Bible is gradually eroded to the point that it disappears altogether. At the end of the day, so to speak, the theologians (the so-called experts!) determine what is an essential core, or non-essential packaging.

Making Distinctions

An astute theologian in the Reformed churches, the late Rev. Johannes Francke, provided us with a valuable insight about how we must read and interpret Scripture. "When Paul states in 1 Cor. 11:4 that he wants women to pray with covered

---

4. Synodical Reformed Church - In 1944, the Reformed Churches (Liberated) - GKv - liberated themselves from the decisions of the general synod and established a new identity. Collectively they continued to uphold the Church Order of Dort. This church order stresses the sovereignty of the local church, cooperating within a federation of churches. Classes, Regional Synods and General Synods are seen as broader assemblies, not higher assemblies. In the synodical Reformed Church, the 'broader' assemblies function in a hierarchical form of government.

5. Hermeneutics is the science of exegesis (or the explanation) of Scripture. Basic to Reformed hermeneutics is the notion that the Scriptures do not contradict themselves, and that the Scriptures themselves provide the information we need to explain Scriptures. Contemporary hermeneutics has added another criterion: the cultural context in which one reads the Bible. For example, Paul's historical, societal context was significantly different from ours, therefore our interpretation must be gauged to the context of our time. In short, contemporary culture must be a "lens' through which we read the Bible.

6. Readers may wonder why this process in the synodical churches is profiled in this chapter. On the North American continent, the Christian Reformed Churches (CRCNA) have experienced a similar development, albeit 20 to 30 years later.

heads, and then in 1 Cor. 14:35 when he says that '*it is disgraceful (ugly) for a woman to speak in the church,*' is he simply accommodating his thinking to the customs of his time?"

We must make some distinctions here. Francke writes:
> In 1 Cor. 14:34 where Paul commands women in the congregation to be silent, and in 1 Tim. 2:12 where he forbids women to teach in the congregation (i.e., perform the work of a pastor and teacher) and forbids them to rule over men (i.e., rule in the congregation as an elder), I cannot see why these commands should be seen as time-bound prescriptions. The apostle forbids these matters, not because it is shameful that a woman would speak in the congregation, as such. But he says this because it is the result of the creational order. That particular argument is first mentioned in 1 Tim. 2:13, highlighting the fall into sin (vs. 14) and again in 1 Cor. 14:34. Only then does he say it is "disgraceful" or "shameful". Why is this shameful? Because the speaking he refers to is a transgression of the 'law' (vs. 34ff). It is quite clear that pertinent to this imposition of 'silence', Paul appealed to the creational order.

How must we read his injunction about the covered head in 1 Cor. 11:33ff? Wasn't that simply a custom embraced by women in those days? Francke states:
> If we assume that Paul is talking about the head covering of Greek women, then we should remember that Paul sees the head covering in church as a form of deference to the order of creation. That sign (of subordination) can change, but the issue remains: subordination. Therefore, we cannot say that when the sign (head covering) disappears, the issue (of subordination) also disappears. According to Paul, the subordination of the women is expressed by the covered head, remaining silent, not teaching, not ruling.[7]

This normative element is removed if one were to state that Paul is only concerned about the desired mores in his day as these relate to the relationship of men and women. It has also been claimed that deep in his heart, Paul wanted complete equality of men and women, but because of the common practices of his day, the apostle is simply providing the church with a careful suggestion, that the church may use to her advantage many centuries later. This line of reasoning is simply not true. We don't have to look for deeper motives with the writers of the Bible. Instead, we must believe that the Holy Spirit, as the primary Author, has written the Holy Scriptures transparently.

Some interpreters maintain that the text that commands the women to be silent was added later on and therefore not part of Paul's authorship.

7; J. Francke. (1946). The place of the women in the church.

Interpreters have tried in all kinds of ways to change the paragraph in 1 Cor. 14 in such a fashion that it will provide an opening to admit women to the ruling offices of the church. When they do this, they eviscerate Scriptures, and end up declaring that Paul's statements were simply time-bound opinions!

1 Timothy 2: 12

Similar things can be said concerning another critical text in the context of this issue, 1 Tim. 2:12, where the apostle writes, "I do not permit a woman to teach or to assume authority over a man; she must be quiet". In this particular chapter, the apostle is discussing the assembly of the congregation, and especially the prayer in these assemblies. In vs. 8 we read, "Therefore I want the men everywhere to pray, lifting up holy hands without anger or disputing." And in vs. 9, "I also want the women to dress modestly, with decency and propriety." He follows this command with the words, "A woman should learn in quietness and full submission."

The conflicting roles described by Paul are expressed in the words: *"learn in quietness. . ."* as opposed to *"not permit a woman to teach"* What does the apostle mean with "learning" and "teaching"? The first word is a derivative of the Greek word for "disciple or student". Whereas the second word has its root in the concept of "doctrine", a word that occurs more frequently in the pastoral letters (e.g., 2 Tim. 4: 2, ". . . and encourage —with great patience and careful instruction." Also, in Titus 1: 9, where Paul urges Titus that "he must hold firmly to the trustworthy message as it has been taught, so that he can encourage others by sound doctrine.") In the Greek text, Paul uses two words that are used for *doctrine*, both derived from the word "instruction" that we read in 1 Tim. 2:12. More examples could be given but it is clear that *teaching*, or instruction, the admonition of the congregation, is not the task of women.

The apostle Paul does not permit a woman to teach the congregation or that she would use Scripture to admonish the congregation, especially admonitions about ethical issues.

This prohibition does beg the question: is it possible that a woman would be permitted to carry out the proclamation of the complete gospel? After all, ethical issues and admonitions only constitute (a small) part of the complete task of proclaiming the gospel. Also, it seems to be reasonable to factor in the differences between the gathering of the congregation in Paul's day as compared to ours today. To illustrate the absurdity of this presumed (false) dilemma, someone suggested the following analogy: Imagine if someone has been forbidden to consume *dessert*, would it be reasonable to assume that it would be o.k. if he would eat the *complete dinner*?

The apostle provides two arguments in support of his prohibition: His first argument is rooted in creation: "For Adam was formed first, then Eve," (1 Tim. 2:13). Paul asserts that the order that God established in the creation of man and woman is definitive and determinative: the woman may not have authority over the man, and because she may not exercise authority over a man, she does not have authority to admonish. Nor should a woman instruct, or teach the congregation, but rather, she should be open to *be* instructed. This prohibition has nothing to do with a slavish submission, or discrimination that underscores inferiority, but it is entirely based on the place of the woman in the midst of the congregation and the role within the congregational assemblies.

In the second place, Paul states, "And Adam was not the one deceived; it was the woman who was deceived and became a sinner" (vs. 14). This statement raises the question: how can the apostle say that Adam was not misled? Our response must be that Paul does not deny that Adam fell into sin, but we must observe *how* this happened as distinct from Eve's fall into sin. Eve was misled by the serpent; Adam was misled by his wife. The woman functioned as leader of the man but ended being his *misleader*. Eve submitted to Satan's temptation; Adam fell into sin through the transgression of his wife.

Paul presents this as irrefutable proof: these are the grounds that the apostle uses to draw his conclusion with respect to the role of women in worship services: women are not to admonish, but instead, they should remain silent.

Does that mean that women are completely relegated to the lowest ranks? May they not serve in the 'office of all believers' (cf. Lord's Day 12, q. & a. 32[8])? The last verse of this chapter is important in this context: "But women will be saved through childbearing—if they continue in faith, love and holiness with propriety" (1 Timothy 2:15). Women are also anointed with the Holy Spirit, which means that they must "continue in faith" in fulfilling their task in love, sanctified through the Holy Spirit.

What, specifically, is the task of women? Paul is quite definitive: the family. Her sanctification, her salvation (in Greek: the unfolding of her life, or purpose), is in bringing children into the world. That's her greatest and most important task: promoting the coming of the kingdom by populating the new earth. Of course, this task would also include raising children as mother. She must carry out this task

---

8. Q. Why are you called a Christian? (Heidelberg Catechism, Lord's Day 12, Question & Answer 32)
A. Because I am a member of Christ by faith and thus share in his anointing, so that I may as prophet confess his name, as priest present myself a living sacrifice of thankfulness to him, and as king fight with a free and good conscience against sin and the devil in this life, and hereafter reign with him eternally over all creatures.

"with propriety," i.e., maintaining self-control. Women must not rule over men, but they must maintain control (i.e., rule) over themselves.

OFFICES

It is clear in 1 Tim. 2 that Paul is writing about married women, similar to 1 Cor. 11. That prompts a question: what about single women?

In Paul's letters, we observed that he outlined a specific task for widows, as he also does for unmarried women, a task that is similar to several women mentioned in his letters. Concerning the special offices in Christ's church, women are not mentioned; men are.

It's striking that after 1 Tim. 2:12, Paul writes about the requirements of office. We may even conclude that these requirements are described in contrast to each other: the ministry of women in contrast to the ministry of men. It is an outstanding task that women continue in faith, love and sanctification, with propriety. But if a man aspires to fulfill the task of overseer, he desires an "noble" calling. And subsequently, Paul lists the qualifications of office.

Included in these qualifications is the requirement that a man is husband of *one* wife (not more). Additionally, he must "manage his family well and see that his children obey him, and he must do so in a manner worthy of full respect" (vs. 4).

Deacons must also be the husband of one wife. They too must manage their family and their children well. Clearly, office-bearers must manage their households well and they must be faithful to their wives. Concerning office-bearers, the apostle states that their wives must be "worthy of respect, not malicious talkers but temperate and trustworthy in everything" (vs. 11). These qualifications show that Paul's instruction in 1 Tim. 2 runs parallel to 1 Tim. 3. There is no hint or suggestion that there is room for women in the ruling offices. Neither is there any room for the interpretation that when Paul writes about the wives of deacons, that he would mean women as deacons. The earlier verse clearly writes about a man as deacon: he may only have one wife and he is the head of his family.

When we carefully consider the above issues, we are able to establish a clear connection to 1 Tim. 5, where the apostle describes the station of a particular category of women, the widows. In chapter 5, he speaks about another side of the gender issue: that the woman (widow) has been the wife of one man. "No widow may be put on the list of widows unless she is over sixty, . . ." In Greek, Paul uses an expression from which we derive our word "catalogue".

The widows Paul references are put on a list. This word indicates an organized ministry that also existed after the time of the apostles. This ministry involved ministering to those in need and the nursing of the sick. This task was not, however, part of the special offices which Paul describes in his Pastoral Letters. That special office, to which men of Christ's church may aspire, is clearly set apart from the service of the silent, ministering, servant task of the married and unmarried women in the church.

10. Voting Rights in the Church?

Consequences?

In chapter 9, I argued that sources in the New Testament, especially 1 Cor. 14 and 1 Tim. 2, prohibit the admission of women to the ruling offices in the church of Jesus Christ. Our wise God deemed it appropriate to reserve the special offices of the church for men who are equipped with gifts to serve the church.

Does this limitation mean that women must be excluded from the 'office of all believers'? Absolutely not. In both the Old and New Testaments there is abundant evidence that there is a valued and rich task for women. Remember what the apostle Paul writes in Galatians 3:28: "There is neither Jew nor Gentile, neither slave nor free, nor is there male and female, for you are all one in Christ Jesus". To Timothy, Paul writes that women should "continue in faith, love and holiness with propriety" (1 Tim. 12:15). The common faith in Jesus Christ binds men and women together; the mutual bond of love toward Christ also connects them. In a similar fashion, men and women share in the grace of the Holy Spirit who sanctifies our whole life to be focussed on God's honour.

But if women may not be chosen to serve in the ruling offices in Christ's church, how must we view the involvement of women in voting for office-bearers? Within the congregation, may they give voice to their choice by actively voting? It has often been stated that if the one is not possible neither should the other. Women who may not become ministers (in a teaching office), elder (ruling office) or deacon, should not be permitted to participate in choosing others to fill that office.

Many people firmly maintain their opposition: if you permit women to participate in actively voting for office-bearers, then the next step will be the admission of women to the ruling offices themselves, an argument based on fear of the slippery slope. A church that allows women to vote for office-bearers will without any question, end up admitting women to the ruling offices of the church, including ministers on the pulpit. The view that has been presented to the congregation hangs like a sword of Damocles[1] above the congregation, cultivating the notion that this 'first' step is irrevocably associated with a host of other dangers to Biblical orthodoxy: beware! Without any question, once you've taken this step, it's a forgone conclusion that soon women will be admitted to all the ruling offices of the church!

Fear of the inevitability of a slippery slope is used as an argument to prevent what the critics see as the ultimate conclusion of this matter: women in office. Their conclusion? Why even consider going down that road?

Argumentation

Fear is a poor councillor. People who live that way see all kinds of dangers and problems, and as a result, they will never try anything new. Those who embrace such an attitude must consider Eccles. 11: 4: "Whoever watches the wind will not plant; whoever looks at the clouds will not reap." The question arises: what leads people to embrace such reasoning? Let's try to unpack this thinking.

In their reasoning they conclude that the apostle commands that in the church, a woman may not rule over a man and she may not have authority over a man. Those who are called to the ruling offices of the church are given authority; they must govern. People who participate in the elections for office-bearers do not actually participate in governing or ruling, but they do participate in a general form of governance. That 'general form of governance' is perceived as a form of ruling, the exercise of authority. Because women are not permitted to exercise authority, they may not participate in the election of office-bearers. In other words, they extend Paul's prohibition to speak/teach in the congregation (1 Cor. 14: 34; 1 Tim. 2: 12) to the process of the election of office-bearers.[2]

---

1. According to the story, Damocles was a Greek courtier in the court of King Dionysius II in Syracuse in 4th century B.C. He proclaimed that the king was fortunate to have such power and riches. Dionysius traded places with him for a day. Damocles was surrounded by all the things he had claimed were so great, but Dionysius had hung a sword above his head, suspended by a horse hair, symbolic of all the challenges and enemies that threatened the king.

2. The issue allowing women to vote for office-bearers has been discussed at several general synods of the Canadian Reformed Churches. The argumentation presented above was often used by the opponents to women's voting rights. At the General Synod of Dunnville (2016) of the Canadian Reformed Churches the decision was made to leave this issue in the freedom of the churches.

In the past, the Reformed church embraced the opinion that participation in the election of office-bearers was *not* advisory, but rather an act of general governance, as distinguished from special governance which Christ invested the special office of the overseers. Therefore, Reformed synods in the past decided not to accede to the request to allow women members of the church to vote for office-bearers.

How did the men at general synods derive at this conclusion? The answer lies in the philosophical views that had been taught by Dr. Abraham Kuyper.[3] His views led to a fragmentation of the office of all believers which Christ had endowed upon men and women alike. In matters of election, only men could participate because they participated in a form of general governance (exercising authority) in the choice of elders and deacons.

Before and after the election

In many churches there is an established tradition that before the election of a minister, or of elders and deacons, the congregation, (i.e., men and women), is given the opportunity to submit names of men whom the congregation considers suitable for office. The *congregation*, that is comprised of both communicant men and women, is requested to consider this matter and then submit names.

After the elections have taken place, the announcement is made that if no lawful objections are submitted, the following brothers will be installed in their respective offices. Both men and women are requested to provide the ruling council with any legal objections against the ordination, a process called *approbation* (providing informed consent or objection). For example, if a woman in the congregation were to judge that a certain brother, (who has been appointed to become elder or deacon), should not be ordained as office-bearer by the consistory, it is her task to express her objection to the consistory. If her reasons are sound, then the consistory is obliged to listen to her and follow through with her objections.

No one has raised an issue that the tasks preceding and following the election of office-bearers is shared by both brothers and sisters in the congregation. In fact, the process of approval of, or objection to the elected office-bearers by both men and women was affirmed by the synod of Arnhem (1930). In other words,

---

3. As mentioned earlier, Dr. Kuyper was an imposing figure in the Reformed churches in the late 19th century and the early 20th century. This influence had a major impact on the Reformed churches in both theological as well as philosophical respects. One of Kuyper's theories pertained to his views on God's grace. All humanity benefited from common grace (rain, the fruit of the land, the benefits of human intelligence, etc.). Particular grace was reserved for God's children.
Kuyper also embraced a similar view of the offices in the church. He wrote about the special or particular office in the church, evident in the ruling and teaching offices of the church, and the general offices, or the office of all believers. Church members in the latter office are called to vote for office-bearers, for example. Though the office of all believers is for men and women, the voting for office-bearers is deemed to be part of the general office or general governance of the church but was only 'reserved' for communicant male members of the congregation.

in the context of the overall governance of the congregation, it is accepted that women have a legitimate role in the submitting of names of suitable men, and subsequently, in the provision of consent or objection. But women were/are not permitted to have a voice in actually voting/electing (i.e., choosing) men for office.

In conclusion: the task of the sisters in the congregation in the context of the overall governance of the congregation, is fragmented. They have no task in the special office of governance. That task was to be restricted to men, but in the overall governance of the congregation she does share in the task of approbation.

This scholastic hairsplitting of general/overall governance that excludes women from the governance in the form of elections is inconsistent and absurd, a remnant of Kuyperian scholasticism.

Is voting exercising authority?

What is the big question that has confronted many synods in the past: is participation in an election exercising authority? The apostle prohibits women from exercising authority over the men. Is that truly the case when women participate in the election of office-bearers? Many people still maintain that it is. These people argue as follows: people who vote, speak. And for women that is forbidden because the apostle has clearly stated that the woman must be silent in the congregation, across the board. Women are said to be ruling, exercising authority over men.

Just imagine (they say) if a women's husband was one of the candidates, and imagine that the vote of that one sister ended up being critical in the election. Imagine that she decided to vote for another man, not her husband. In that case, she would be deemed to be ruling over her husband. Therefore, a woman must not participate in the election of office-bearers.

No, voting in elections is not exercising authority. Remember that the church council appoints the men to office. This same body of officers is not dependent on the decision of the congregation, whether that is only the male communicant members or both male and female members. The consistory makes the appointments, or one could also say that the consistory 'calls' the brothers to office. By means of the mediation of the congregation, i.e., the election (voting by the congregation), consistory executes this decision. People who want to substitute the word 'speaking' for the word 'voting', create a very questionable change in the understanding of voting, by suggesting that this process is the same as the one described in 1 Tim. 2: 12. In this reference, the apostle is writing about speaking *to* the congregation, an admonition directed *to* the congregation. Voting, or choosing, however, is about speaking *with* or *together with* the congregation. That is an essential distinction because this speaking *with* the congregation also happens in another manner - the worship service by means of songs of praise. Are women excluded from this form of speaking? Of course not!

Is participation in voting or electing a matter of carrying out authority, especially if, for example, a woman would avoid voting for her own husband? The concept of general governance does not fit here, nor does the concept of exercising authority. Exercising authority is what a man/husband does in the context of his marriage. Exercising authority is what office-bearers do over the congregation. Those who choose or elect others to a government, are themselves not part of the government. That is a simple reality, also in the church, though the concept of 'government' may be less applicable in the church context. In contrast, Christ puts more emphasis – especially over against the powers of his day – on *service*, when he addresses the offices in the church.

There are other problems if we consider voting as a form of governing or exercising authority. On the one hand we have the woman who does not want to vote for her husband because she does not want him to become an office-bearer. Some people see that as a form of exercising authority – albeit, over her husband. But on the other hand, think of the many young communicant members, some who have not even reached official adulthood, and still live under the supervision and authority of their parents. When the consistory calls all those entitled to vote, (since they have made public profession of their faith), they too will vote. In fact, we may be thankful if they take their responsibility seriously.

But how must we view the situation if a young man refuses to vote for his own father, if he was a candidate on the slate provided by the consistory? Should we conclude that he exercised authority over his father, which would be in conflict with the 5th commandment? Clearly, from the above examples, it appears that we will come to all kinds of strange consequences if it is assumed that voting for office-bearers is exercising authority.

Would the problem be solved if it were decided that young men should not participate in elections until they are independent or married, and no longer living in the parental home? If the churches were to implement such a strategy, churches would end up having a special group of communicant male members who would function as the electorate, a unique group in the overall governance of the congregation.

Cooperation

With respect to the elections in church, should we accept the existence of an office within the office of all believers, called the office of *overall governance*? No, we should not. The suggestion that such a special office would actually exist has led to the view that voting is a form of ruling, or exercising authority. Actually, the concept as such, is irrelevant. Election of office-bearers is all about the cooperation of the members of the congregation.

When the church council establishes a slate of candidates, it does not state that one candidate will be a better office-bearer than the other. No, they state that all the men on the slate are considered to have the gifts to serve as elder or deacon. The council simply asks the congregation for their assistance as believers to choose their preference. Not to forget, however, both men and women are mature believers in the congregation of Jesus Christ. At this point, remember the distinctions! Women are called upon more often to provide their assistance. In the Old Testament, we observed that the involvement of women was incidental, but in the New Covenant they are called upon regularly as co-workers in the church, co-gifted with the anointing of the Holy Spirit.

Where does the concept or the term, 'male communicant members' have its origin? Do those men represent the congregation? That can be said of the church council/consistory of the congregation; they represent the congregation. In elections, however, the council requests the cooperation of the congregation, before, during and after the elections. Names are submitted, voting takes place and the approbation of the appointed brothers is requested. Some people may subscribe to the tradition of using only the male communicant members; it's always been that way. That is, however, a weak defence.

In earlier synodical reports, it was argued that Scriptures repeatedly and exclusively write about 'brothers.' That, too, is untenable. A Reformed minister[4] early in the 20th century (1927) stated, "When the apostles address the *whole* congregation, they normally used the address, "brothers", (see Rom. 1: 13; 7: 1; 10: 1; 1 Cor. 2: 1; 3: 1, etc.). The sisters are specifically addressed when he has an issue that is particularly for the women. The address of the women is always included in the address of the men, as seen in the salutations and blessings in their letters. Lindeboom maintains that they assumed that women are included with the men.

---

4. Rev. Cornelis Lindeboom, (1872 - 1938), an early proponent of allowing women to vote in elections of office-bearers, in a public presentation at the seminary in Kampen (1905). His proposal met with stiff opposition.

Men are addressed first, but women were included in the address to 'men' (i.e., brothers). For example, in the salutations or greetings, and the blessings: the saints (Rom. 1: 7; Eph. 1: 1; the saints in Christ Jesus in 1 Cor. 1: 2) where Paul consistently addresses the masculine gender. He addresses the *whole* congregation, also its female members whom he addresses as 'brothers' or with other words, always using the masculine gender. The apostles subsume women in the address of the men, but not with the intention that the women 'disappear' behind the identity of the men. Such reasoning would mean that women would lose the recognition of their unique rights and duties, their work and honour. What Paul says in Eph. 6 to the fathers (vs. 4), the servants/slaves (vs. 5), the men (vs. 9), is equally applicable for the mothers, maid-servants and women.

Is there even one admonition directed to 'brothers', that is not equally directed to the 'sisters'? When Paul says in Eph. 6: 10, *"Finally, my brethren, be strong in the Lord, and in the power of his might,"* (KJV), or in 1 Thess. 5: 25, *"Brothers, pray for us. Greet all the brothers with a holy kiss"* (ESV), would he not also include the female members of the congregation? Would anyone dare to suggest that on the basis of James 5:9, *"Do not grumble against one another, brothers, so that you may not be judged"*, that the grumbling of the sisters would be acceptable?

Acts 6 also provides us with support for our argument to include women in the election process. In verse 5, (ESV) we read, *"And what they said pleased the whole gathering, and they chose Stephen, a man full of faith and of the Holy Spirit."* The whole gathering, Luke says, that is both men and women.

In the discussion about women's participation in electing office-bearers, are women transgressing Biblically imposed restrictions when they (as communicant members) vote for office-bearers? Do they cross Biblically imposed boundaries when they participate in meetings of the congregation where other church matters are discussed: the church finances, or other matters concerning church life? Is it against Paulinian prohibitions when women, communicant members committed to the Lord, participate in the discussion or make suggestions? Of course not!

Clearly efforts have been made to establish a boundary based on the facts in Scripture. If that is done, then it should be done using proper criteria, otherwise in the future, in different situations, it will be even more difficult to determine the Scriptural role of women in the Lord's service. That it's justified to have women express themselves, asking questions or making comments or suggestions, at meetings of the congregation, should not be misconstrued to suggest that therefore it is also justified that women administer God's Word in the congregation. If sisters in the congregation are permitted to vote, we should not jump to the conclusion that they do so in a ruling capacity and therefore they should also be permitted to become ruling elders and deacons.

The calling that believers have, should not be confused with the responsibility of the offices in Christ's church, the office of the ministry of God's Word or the offices of elder or deacon. Active participation of the sisters in a meeting of the congregation, in a variety of ways, including voting for office-bearers, is a matter of cooperation with the congregation. As communicant members, they can be involved in all kinds of ways. Together with their husbands (for those who are married), they work together in the place that Christ has placed them.

NOT LIMITED

The service of women in church should not be limited to the issue of women's voting! What beautiful and important tasks there are in the church of Christ in the context of the office of all believers! The Lord wants to engage her talents of head, heart and hands, in service to the King of the church and in the interest of his kingdom and his will.

In Christ, the basis of the paradisal order has been restored. That means that men must lead, and women join in and help. And certainly, that does not mean that men, as 'extroverts', work with their focus to the outside, and that women should be introverted and focussed on the hearth and home. God leads both men and women back to their former calling to work together, to cultivate creation to God's glory. Christ wants to use *both* for the kingdom of his Father. For the church that means that women, in the calling of all believers, are called to be assistants to the office-bearers.

What does this look or sound like? Think of the practical implications in the context of the communion of saints, where women can use their gifts and talents given by the LORD. They can be such wonderful and supportive co-workers, also in their outreach with the gospel. Equipped with their knowledge of the gospel, they can bring comfort and encouragement in their outreach to the lonely, the aged, the needy. What a comfort they may bring by a word of encouragement, discussions about the riches of faith in Christ, by providing Christian advice! Wherever there is a family in distress, wherever people are waiting for the supportive role of a sister in the congregation, these women who embrace the role of encouragement and support, provide much more than simply providing an extra set of hands in a family.

The form of assistance can be so meaningful especially in a spiritual sense. Think of the faith, the love and sanctification that Paul describes, specifically in connection with women in the congregation. That assistance is not limited to families, but may also radiate its goodness beyond the family and the church, to those outside the communion of saints. Women in the congregation may also confess the name of God, i.e., openly and publicly confess his name, engaging their talents in service to God's church and kingdom. In their struggle against sin in their lives, visible in so many places, they will show the power of faith!

Elders would do well to encourage deacons to motivate women to provide and organize these women's ministries.

II. Conclusion

In the first chapter of this booklet, I described the spirit of emancipation that has (re)moved many traditional boundaries and many of the accepted limitations established by God. Women must be liberated from all the restraining impositions that have held them back! This spirit of emancipation also threatens God's children, in marriage relationships and family life, their relationship to the church and the kingdom of God. When we make assumptions that the Bible is perhaps culturally time-bound, we will end up in an endless debate trying to determine the limitations of these cultural limitations.

We've observed that the secular forces in society want to liberate women from all constraints and provide them with a form of freedom that has essentially become lawlessness, freedom *from* the law of God. It is therefore the obligation of the church to preach the liberty of women directed in the service of, and in service to the Lord, *consistent* with the demands of service to God. This preaching requires a renewed reflection about the definition of boundaries in our service to the LORD, also the boundaries for women. There's no room for revolution or foolish progressivism, no room for uncontrolled emancipation. Rather, we must be driven by a Biblical renewal of our Reformed thinking.

Such thinking strives to maintain a Scriptural balance, by avoiding the extremes of uncontrolled progressivism on the one hand, and the stranglehold of blinded conservativism on the other hand that swears allegiance to tradition for the sake of tradition. The church, which is a living body of living members must avoid becoming fossilized, rigid.

In accordance with the old paradisal order, (which will be fully restored upon Christ's return), men and women may work together to execute the culture mandate, their calling to maintain and develop this world. The world at large is the grand workshop in which the church has been placed. Therefore, God's children, men and women alike, must be mobilized to continue the great struggle to promote God's kingdom in the face of the sinful challenges of this world that bristles with animosity. We work until the Bride appears. On that great day, he will invite his faithful workers to the great wedding feast, all the men and women, boys and girls, brothers and sisters who eagerly looked forward to his appearing.

12. Reflection & Discussion

For the purpose of reflection and discussion, participants should use a notebook to record their thoughts, especially how these relate to Biblical truths. Depending on the discussion setting (church or home) other materials may be helpful if they are available:
- Chart paper, masking tape to post the papers
- Laptop computer, LCD projector and a suitable projection surface

Successful discussion requires a collaborative attitude that includes *active listening*, i.e., listening to understand *why* people say what they do. If we try to understand their motivation we will be equipped to understand them rather than simply score debating points.

Participants should also have their Bibles available, either a hardcopy or a digital version.

Emancipation

We live in the 21st century, more than one hundred years after women in most western countries were given the right to own property and vote in civic elections. The freedoms women have today, and the lifestyles they may choose today are in shrill contrast to the place of women less than one hundred years ago. Take a large piece of chart paper and draw three columns as illustrated on the next page.

REFLECT ON THE FOLLOWING

	Society at large	My church community
The role and service of women in the family.		
Personal reflections – what are the Biblical challenges?		
Educational opportunities for women.		
Personal reflections – what are the Biblical challenges?		
Freedoms we enjoy – compared to e.g., Muslim countries.		
Personal reflections – what are the Biblical challenges?		
Freedoms that are an abuse		
Personal reflections – what are the Biblical challenges?		
Other issues?		

MALE AND FEMALE HE CREATED THEM

1. What is the symbolic significance of woman's creation from a rib of Adam? Why did God not make Eve as he made Adam: i.e., formed from a separate piece of clay?

2. How did the creation of Eve impact on the role that Eve had with Adam before the Fall?

3. Is Eve's being *different* to be interpreted as unequal to Adam? Did the difference also include a subordinate role for woman? (Remember: this is before the Fall.)

4. Try to imagine what the role and relationship of Adam and Eve would have been like if they had not fallen into sin. How may that relationship have grown over time also between the genders of Adam's/Eve's posterity? (Note what the apostle Paul says about gender relations.)

5. Even after the Fall, men and women remained image bearers of God. What are the attributes of being an image-bearer?
For men and women, regardless of gender?
For men?
For women?

6. If you believe gender distinctions are not part of image bearing, explain why you think so. Are there Scripture references that support this idea?

7. In 1 Timothy 2:13-15, Paul writes: "For Adam was formed first, then Eve. And Adam was not the one deceived; it was the woman who was deceived and became a sinner. But women will be saved through childbearing—if they continue in faith, love and holiness with propriety." Summarize what Dr. Deddens writes about this text. Explain what the implications are for men and women believers in church today.
What does this text mean for single women?

8. If a woman believes she has a special gift (in music, medicine, etc.) and decides that she cannot pursue motherhood without jeopardizing the development of this special gift, what must she do?

9. Some exegetes stress that Jesus Christ's redemption of both men and women also covered Eve's sin of rebellion in paradise and therefore Paul's injunction appears to conflict with God's grace? How would you explain that problem?

By Godly ordinance or by chance?

1. When tempted by the devil, Eve reiterated God's command about the Tree of Knowledge of Good and Evil (and even added to it: "you shall not touch it"). She then listened to the promises of the devil. She held knowledge of God's truth and the devil's lie – how would you describe her sin at that point? (*cf.* Was it right for her to listen to two options as though they were equal and then make a judgement?)

2. Eve gives some of the fruit to her husband and he eats. What are the immediate consequences?

3. What evidence of treatment towards women and children does Dr. Deddens provide regarding the curse as articulated to Eve after the Fall? He refers to these evidences under the heading *paganism*.

4. How much different is the description about centuries ago than your understanding of Western Civilization only a few hundred years ago or even modern day Islam?

5. Why would abortion on demand be a sign of a low view of women, as described by the Greeks.

6. We might wish to think that the Jews' treatment of women was in stark contrast with what was experienced by them among pagan cultures. Dr. Deddens makes it clear that this was not the case.

7. In what ways was it evident that Jews also treated women unfairly?
Is this treatment of women sin, or is it justified because Eve was the one who was tempted and gave some fruit to her husband? Do women deserve this treatment because of the Fall?

Women in the Old Testament

1. Despite the sinful treatment of women by the Old Testament community, what evidences, in general, does Dr. Deddens find in the Old Testament that testify to the standards and high regard that the Lord provided for women?

2. The story of the daughters of Zelophehad provides a number of important points that demonstrate how women were to be treated within the Old Testament community. There are implications regarding marriage, inheritance, and spiritual inheritance. Discuss these implications and any others that you can discern from the text.

3. In what way does Miriam serve as a prophetess?

4. Why is it significant that Miriam was punished for her rebellion?

5. What, if any, particular attributes of Deborah made her a suitable leader in Israel? Dr. Deddens wants to make it clear to us that Deborah is not seeking to be 'emancipated' – what is his point in making this evident?

6. After discussing the example of Hulda, Dr. Deddens concludes the chapter:
   These women were not chattels or slaves, but neither were they champions of emancipation. They were ordained to serve in the coming of our Lord, Jesus Christ. It was this service that typified these women in the Old Testament.
   Are we to understand that some women had a formal office in the Old Testament?

7. Dr. Deddens mentions a contrast between being a "chattel or slave" and being "emancipated". How would you understand the two extremes that Deddens is contrasting?

Spiritual Maturity – Pentecost

1. When looking at all the evidence that Dr. Deddens provides in this chapter, what conclusions would you reach about:
   - the role of men and women in the church?
   - the role of mothers and fathers in the family (i.e., Covenantal headership)?
   - the difference between how women were treated in the Old Testament community and how that treatment is (or should be) different in the New Testament community.

2. The service of several women mentioned in Paul's letters
   Euodia and Syntyche were actively involved in helping the church spreading God's Word. Deddens describes their work as 'the special service of women'. In fact, he concludes: *These women had been called to a lofty service in God's kingdom, to help the church spread God's Word, the preaching of the gospel, the message of salvation!*
   How could women (and all members in the pew) be involved in sharing the gospel without the formal office of missionary, minister, or elder?

3. How does Phoebe serve as an example of Godliness to women in the New Testament church?

4. Priscilla and her husband Aquila were active and engaged members of the early church. Why is it significant that Priscilla is often mentioned first when the couple is introduced? How do Priscilla and Aquila demonstrate a love for Christ's church and serve as a model to Christian couples today?

5. In the early church, women were engaged in much more than nursing the sick or other forms of mercy, as outlined by Deddens. Discuss how the women in scripture, and women today, fulfill the three-fold office of Christians as prophetess, priestess, and queen (*cf.* prophet, priest, and king).

A Contradiction in the Bible?

Chapter 7 deals with a pretty complicated and challenging number of texts. Dr. Deddens seeks to demonstrate how seemingly contradictory texts on the role of women in the teaching role of the church can be complementary, not contradictory.

After reading through the chapter, how do you perceive Deddens' explanation of the understanding that women are to be silent in the church and that they are to prophesy with their heads covered?

Other Developments with Respect to the Role of Women

The Order or Class of Widows is introduced in this chapter using the latin *viduat*.
1. Describe and discuss the tasks and role of the women belonging to this Order in the early Christian church?

2. In the 4th Century, many changes began taking place and the role of deaconesses was quickly limited or even abolished, first in the Western and then in the Eastern churches. Can you think of reasons as to why this happened? How did the church become increasingly patriarchical?

3. After the Middle Ages continued to denigrate the role of women in society and in the church, the Reformation began to restore the role of women. In particular, Luther and Calvin stressed the blessing of Godly women serving among the saints. Discuss Luther's comment about women preaching, and Calvin's comment about women diaconate.

4. Rev. Heldring set up a home for former prostitutes among other charitable activities. Do you know of any Reformed churches that have done something similar? Is there a connection between increased doctrinal orthodoxy and a decreased emphasis on the ministry of mercy, especially outside of the church?

5. Dr. Abraham Kuyper encouraged allowing women a voice in politics and to permit them voting rights. Is it true that voting by secret ballot can encourage secrecy between a husband and his wife? And if so, is that a problem among Christians within society, or within the church?

6. Modern movements want to see equality of women within the church to mean equality of opportunity to serve in the formal offices of the church. There has been a correlation between society's view of women and the church's treatment of women. Today's emancipation movement would demand that women's take on the ruling offices of the church. Deddens concludes this chapter with: *There is a difference between unscriptural emancipation and Scriptural reformation!*
Are you able to articulate those differences?

Women in the Ruling Offices of the Church?

One of the big questions about permitting women in the formal offices of the church has to do with hermeneutical thinking (page 65, footnote 3).

What is meant by hermeneutics, and what changes take place in hermeneutics to make room for women in office?

Women's Voting

Deddens concludes that women's participation in the voting for office-bearers is appropriate because it is not the exercise of authority. Various churches have struggled with this question in the past.

Why might some struggle with the idea women participating in the voting of office-bearers? Why might others struggle with the idea of women not being permitted to participate?

General Question

In chapter 8 Dr. Deddens described the work of deaconesses in the early church. Would it benefit the church if we were to return to formally inducting capable women into such a ministry of service? Recognizing that there are only two offices (elder and deacon) and that these offices are to be filled by men, how could this be done in your current church structure and governance?

(e.g., Consistory and deacons often appoint members to various committees to help with the administration of church life. Could that happen within the Ministry of Mercy, too?)

Photo credits/copyright

- pg. 16 jh-isings.nl
- pg. 22 ucatholic.com
- pg. 28 medieval.eu/women-in-the-medieval-monastic-world/
- pg. 36 wisconsinchristiannews.com
- pg. 42 Wikipedia Commons
- pg. 48 Ben White - Unsplash
- pg. 54 spectator.com.au
- pg. 64 Priscilla Du Preez - Unsplash
- pg. 82 Kelly Sikkema - Unsplash

www.ingramcontent.com/pod-product-compliance
Lightning Source LLC
Chambersburg PA
CBHW051956290426
44110CB00015B/2259